Title page

D0022034

In the Matter of Edwin Potter:

Mental Illness and Criminal Justice Reform

(Based upon a true story)

by

David E. Geiger, M.E.E., P.E.

Copyright

Publisher's Cataloging-In-Publication Data
(Prepared by The Donohue Group, Inc.)

Names: Geiger, David E. | Geiger, David E. Reducing recidivism.
Title: In the matter of Edwin Potter : mental illness and criminal
      justice reform / by David E. Geiger, M.E.E., P.E.
Description: [Wayne, New Jersey] : [David E. Geiger], [2016] |
      "Based upon a true story." | Includes a separately published
      article by the author.
Identifiers: ISBN 978-0-692-79782-2 | ISBN 978-0-692-79788-4
      (ebook)
Subjects: LCSH: Geiger, David E.--Trials, litigation, etc. | Mentally
      ill offenders--United States. | Schizophrenics--Effect of
      imprisonment on. | Criminal justice, Administration of--
      United States. | Uxoricide--United States.
Classification: LCC HV9304 .G45 2016 (print) | LCC HV9304
      (ebook) | DDC 364.80973--dc23

Cover Design and Illustration

Cover design by Jennafer Dufour Barstow

Cover portrait by David E. Geiger

Cover photograph by Peter Cerf

Story Type

Although this story is not a documentary, it is based upon a true story. All of the names have been changed.

Dedication

This book is dedicated to all of those who believed in me, especially my immediate family and "Lucinda Tanzer" who brought our daughter to visit. But it is especially in loving memory of Herma Darrow, MSN, RN who always put the patient first but died of brain cancer and never lived to see this book, her legacy, come about.

Glossary

Recidivist from the Oxford American Dictionary:

A person who constantly commits crimes and seems unable to be cured of criminal tendencies, a persistent offender.

Schizophrenia from the DSM 5:

Schizophrenia is characterized by delusions, hallucinations, disorganized speech and behavior, and other symptoms that cause social or occupational dysfunction. For a diagnosis, symptoms must have been present for six months and include at least one month of active symptoms.

About the Author

David Geiger is a native of New Jersey where he still resides and is married with three grown children. He is an electrical engineer with a baccalaureate degree with honor as well as a master's degree from Stevens Institute of Technology. He has a professional license from the State of New Jersey and worked in New York City for twenty years as an engineer with Con Edison. He is also a member of Mensa where he started his writing interests in *Imprint: The Newsletter of Northern New Jersey Mensa* as of December 1990.

As part of his effort to reduce recidivism he attends conferences at John Jay College of Criminal Justice in New York City. He has a strong interest in music and a love for art which he continues to study at The School of Visual Arts, also in New York City. Some of his work can be seen in the book.

And he still has schizophrenia which has been in full remission, meaning symptom-free, since 2001.

Acknowledgements

Ann Jacobs (Director, Prisoner Re-entry Institute at John Jay College of Criminal Justice) – for allowing me to take part in the conversation

Marni Nachman – for love, support, and marrying me

Alex Keoskey, Esq. – for support and encouragement

Peter Cerf, PB and J Consulting – photography, line editing and friendship

Barbara Cerf, PB and J Consulting – marketing and friendship

Jarod Cerf, PB and J Consulting – editing, web design and friendship

Table of Contents

Part 1 portrays the tragedy of having schizophrenia. Edwin Potter is a young, married, middle-class, home-owning professional. In his delusion, Edwin kills his wife, thinking he is saving her, and is arrested and committed to a maximum security psychiatric facility pending his recovery and trial for his life.

Part 2: The Trial 77
Edwin stands trial for his life and is acquitted as insane. What goes on behind the scenes from the accused's point of view.

Part 3: Release from State Psychiatric Hospital 105
Part 3 concentrates primarily upon life in a maximum security psychiatric facility. Edwin struggles for his freedom. The Prosecutor, who fought so hard to prove Edwin's sanity at the trial, now argues that he is a menace to society and must remain in maximum security.

Part 4:   Release from County Psychiatric Hospital 149

Part 4 opens with the murder of the Director of the maximum security facility at State. Concentrates on life in County and gradual loosening of the restrictions placed upon Edwin as part of his re-integration into society. Here he meets his future mentor Ruth Nussbaum, R.N.

Part 5:   The Struggle to Succeed and the Resulting Relapse 175

This part covers 16 years. Edwin is still a young man but is now on his own in society. Here we begin to see re-entry issues for the mentally ill. He has no direction, but engineering employment and further formal schooling lead to a master's degree and a professional license. This discusses his love life, marriage, new child, divorce, court monitoring, and psychiatric care. He works in New York City as an engineer. He begins his writing career with articles for The High-IQ Society newsletter and starts to win some national awards. Ultimately he experiences relapse and winds up back in County Hospital.

Part 6: Second Release from County Hospital 261

Life in County changed from the first time he was there. The theory of mental illness now is that it is the result of a chemical imbalance. There is still hatred, though, from professionals who should know better. Edwin believes that he has done quite a bit of good despite his illness. Eventually he is released to his parents' supervision.

Art Work by the Author 287

Part 7: The Struggle to Succeed 309

Edwin has matured and has direction in his life now after sitting almost silently for three years in County Hospital. Other re-entry issues manifest themselves at this time. The Global Recession will begin soon, and he finds the Court thwarts him in his search to find a job. He finds love, tries to find a publisher for his book, and we finally see his ground-breaking article "Reducing Recidivism."

Part 8: A Better World 379

This section opens with Edwin's relationship with God which has played a part in the background of the story. Edwin gives his recidivism article to The Criminal Justice College where his recommendations are studied and put into practice in New York City and elsewhere.

Recommended Reading 407

Part 1 (of 8)

The Book of Tears

Chapter 1: Tragedy

Edwin Potter was confused. The problem had been building: things that he had seen, things that he had heard, things that he had remembered. And now it had come to this. Edwin was running desperately down the middle of the street on this summer night.

"Where are they?"

Edwin! – Edwin!

"Where are they?"

Edwin Potter! There is no "they!"

It all looked so... so surreal. The streets were empty. Where was everyone? This was a big city suburb. Why was he alone in the street? Then up ahead a car without its headlights on turned slowly in Edwin's direction. Fear rose in him and brought him to tears.

"They see me! They see me! They'll tell the others! My life is over!"

The car switched on its lights and headed gradually down another street.

Edwin was terrified. He needed to get to his parents' house less than a mile from his own home. He could not take his car. It might have been rigged with explosives that they had put there. So he ran.

"That car! The car I just saw..."

What about the car?

"A co-worker had said something... Yes! Yes! That was it! He said that they would be watching. They were keeping their eyes on me!"

There was a project to be done, and he was the one chosen to make it happen. But he was just a young man! He did not know how to take on a project of that size! Millions of dollars! And it was doomed to failure, but it did not matter. He was the one, and they would torture his young wife and infant son to make him bring it to a successful completion. And they were a mega corporation. They could get what they wanted.

He reached the hill. A light came on at the front porch of one of the houses as he ran passed, and a woman came out quietly. She watched him as he receded up the street, but Edwin focused on his destination – nervous as a cat, knowing that he was running directly into the teeth of the beast. Would he get there? Would they get to him first?

Almost there now. When he reached the house, he threw open the door to the breezeway and almost jumped over to the doorbell and pressed it. No one answered, so he opened the screen door and started to hammer the inside door with his fist. He saw the lights come on. He dropped himself down onto the concrete step and grabbed the hair at the back of his head, but it was already too late. His father came to the door.

"What are you *doing*? What are you kicking the door for?"

What had he done? Edwin had to choose: Should he trust this man? Yes, there was no choice. If this man were a part of their plan, Edwin would lose. If not, they would be waiting for him elsewhere.

Edwin blurted out breathlessly, "I killed my wife and son!"

"What?"

"I killed my wife and son!"

His mother by this time had come to the door.

"What's all this commotion about?"

His father replied in a hushed voice, "He said that he killed Amy and Denny. Call the police! Wait! Call an ambulance first!"

She turned back inside hurriedly.

He bent down and put his arm around his son.

"You didn't hurt anybody! Don't say that! Come inside."

Edwin went into the kitchen and sat in his chair. His father sat in his own chair and kept an eye on his son. Edwin could hear his mother on the telephone in the next room.

In a minute a police car pulled up in the front of the house. Officer Frank Castellano got out and cautiously approached the kitchen door.

"Derek? Mr. Potter?"

"We're in here, Frank."

"How is he?"

"Not well."

"Let's go into the other room and talk. Can your wife watch him?"

"Ellen?"

"Yes?"

"He wants you to watch Edwin for a minute."

"OK."

Edwin watched all of this happen. Was this clean-shaven young man in uniform really a policeman? How much was it costing them to have him come in a squad car to parade as a cop? How far were they willing to go? How big was this plot? Just how important was he – Edwin?

The voices carried on in the other room about bringing him over to the police station and calling the County.

"It might be easier to handle him if you come with us."

"OK."

"OK. Let's see if we can get him to come with us. If there's a problem, we won't force him. I'll call for back-up."

"OK. Let's see what he does."

Edwin's father came back into the kitchen.

"Ed, listen. We have to take you over to the police station. Can you come with us?"

"OK," he answered. He was getting only deeper into the pit. How was he to get out?

Officer Castellano opened the door. Edwin's father took his son by the arm and led him outside.

"Over this way," said his father, guiding Edwin to the squad car. The officer led the way.

Fear gripped Edwin. Would they kill him now? Was his father a part of it? *Was* this his father? He remembered more of what he had heard at work. They told him that the officer – this officer – would come to the house. Then Edwin and his father would be taken to the police station. All of it was coming true.

Officer Castellano opened the rear door of the car, and Edwin got in, followed by his father. The officer shut the door, then went around and got in at the driver's door. He radioed that they were leaving, and they drove quickly to the station. There Edwin and his father were put into a holding cell while the police talked about the status of the situation.

In the cell, Edwin squirmed on the bench so much that his father suggested that he lie on the floor, which he did but to no avail. He tensed up even more. Then all of a sudden, he went limp. And there he lay motionless, his eyes glassy and unblinking.

"Blink your eyes!" his father said uncomfortably, covering them with his hand. Then he called to an officer nearby, "Can you give us a blanket? He must be in shock!"

The officer came over to take a look.

"OK."

Some moments passed before the officer came back with a blanket that Edwin's father put over his son and covered his eyes.

In the meantime, there was some discussion going on at the desk with the County about the action that should be taken at this time. They ascertained that there had been an incident at the home. Both of the injured were admitted to critical care at the local hospital. The result was that the police needed to put Edwin somewhere for the night. He would most probably be arraigned the next day, so the decision was that he would be put in the County jail.

"Derek?" called Officer Castellano.

"Yes?" answered Edwin's father.

"The County is going to pick him up and bring him over to the jail. They'll be here when they get a chance. He said about twenty minutes. I'm sorry."

Chapter 2: Case Opened

When the deputies did arrive from the Sheriff's Department about half an hour later, Edwin was still lying on the floor covered by the blanket with his father seated on the bench above him. The officers discussed Edwin's disposition until they had all of the details.

"Mr. Potter?" called Officer Castellano.

"Yes?"

"You'll have to come out now and let these two officers take him over to the jail."

"All right. Whatever you say."

He shook his son.

"Edwin, I have to go now. We'll see you when they let us. I can't stay any longer. Bye now."

And he backed out of the cell.

One of the officers put the cuffs onto Edwin while the other blocked the door. Then the officer put the leg chains onto Edwin. Edwin saw the guns.

"That's for you," he remembered being told. "No one will know the difference if you are a criminal escaping or they just put you up to it when they shoot you."

Edwin could hardly breathe. Did these men owe them a favor? What did they do for these people so that these men would take him to the worst part of town, shoot him, and leave him there to die? Who would question it if everyone were in on it? There was no escape. If he ran they would all come after him, and he would die anyway.

The memories were endless. They knew what he would do, and they were prepared to deal with it.

One officer took Edwin by the arm, and the three of them walked off to the waiting squad car, got in, and drove away. They drove through some of the worst parts of the city. Edwin prepared himself for death. In a few moments, they were at the County jail. There the garage door opened for them. They pulled in, and the door closed behind them. Here it was: the Valentine's Day massacre.

The officers led him to another cell and put him in with the women. Who were these women? Prostitutes? How should he behave? Maybe it was a test! A test of what? Yes! He remembered what someone had told him, that it would be a test! All of these things were coming true! What kind of test? What else did they say?

He remembered the verse from the gospel of Matthew: *I was in prison and you visited me.* A friend had said it. Edwin remembered. They were checking his resolve to remain pure and holy unto the Lord, to see if he was worthy of being the Messiah. Would he bring the good news of Jesus to those in prison? How, he thought, could he even talk with people from such a different world? He sat immobilized in his chains while the women talked among themselves, glancing at him from time to time.

Some time passed before two guards returned to the cell and called him out. Edwin's chance to evangelize had passed. He had failed. Because of him these women would go to hell – and he along with them for failing to take action. The image grew more intense. Was he a demon? Were they demons? Were all of these people demons dressed as beings of light? How could he tell the difference? What was the test? And who was he? If he were not the Messiah, having failed the test, had he deceived himself for all of his life? Was he not a demon? Maybe he was the antichrist – the devil himself!

Shivers ran up and down his spine. Memories – seeming predictions of the future that were now coming true – just rolled on and on and on.

The guards were now escorting him to an office area where they took off the cuffs for the moment.

"Sit," he was told. So he sat.

"Take all of your personal items out of your pockets. Your glasses too."

Edwin complied. He did not have much: a watch, a wallet, and a set of keys. Glasses, of course. They put the items in a bag and labeled it with his name and a number.

Someone put a yellow form in front of him.

"These are your Miranda rights. Sign it." So he signed it – with difficulty now as they had taken his glasses.

The officer gave Edwin a plastic cup and said, "Go in that room and fill this halfway with urine. Then come back out here."

Edwin did so, returning with the cup.

"Aw for Christ's sake! Leave it in there! I'll get it."

Then there was an intake of his personal information: name, age, street address, next of kin, and so on. Edwin answered the questions. Maybe they were going to write his obituary. His photo with identification number was taken next.

After this was done, the same two guards escorted him to yet another cell, this one with a sink and a toilet but unoccupied. When they reached it they put him inside, took off the chains, closed the gate, and walked away, leaving Edwin alone with his thoughts.

A short time passed before he was composed enough to grieve. He wept bitterly for the longest while, crying out the names of his wife and son over and over again. He had saved them from a fate worse than death. Only he was left now, having failed to kill himself by cutting his own carotid artery. Wondering what was going to happen to him now and finally giving up, he lay down on the bench and fell fitfully asleep.

* * *

Morning broke to the sound of a food tray being pushed under the bars. The fluorescent lights that had been turned off for the night had come back on. Nevertheless, it was impossible to tell what time it was or even if it was night or day. Edwin looked at the plastic tray. There was something that looked like oatmeal, scrambled eggs, a container of some kind of juice, and a spoon. Not understanding why they were feeding him – did Edwin now owe them a favor? – he ate the food, slipped the tray back under the gate, and then sat back on the bench.

Time passed. The memories remained, and he argued with himself about their meaning. There was no escape from this. They had him where they wanted him.

After a while a guard came in to get him. Fearing execution, Edwin asked faintheartedly where he was being taken.

"Population."

Edwin did not know what that was, but it sounded ominous to him. He reached through the bars to plead with the guard.

"Please don't put me out there! They'll kill me -- !"

"DON'T YOU TOUCH ME!" the guard roared. "DON'T YOU EVER TOUCH ME!"

Edwin withdrew hurriedly back behind the bars. The guard left and never returned. Someone came a few minutes later and picked up the tray. Edwin was left to himself again.

A seeming eternity passed before an unimposing bald-headed man dressed in a brown suit and holding a large handful of folders came in and stood in front of Edwin's cell.

"Are you Mr. Potter?"

How does this person know me? Edwin asked himself. Did they send him here?

"Yes."

"I'm Bart Sanders. I'm a public defender. The judge is going to want to make a decision on your case today. How do you want to plead?"

Edwin did not understand. And he had never asked for help in his life. It was time to start. It wasn't going to change anything that they were going to do.

"I-I've never done anything like this. I need help."

Mr. Sanders only stood and looked at him. Then he spoke.

"All right. I'll make the request before the judge."

Then he turned and left, and Edwin was alone with his thoughts once again.

Another eternity passed, and a woman came and stood in front of his cell.

"Edwin?"

Edwin did not recognize this woman.

"Edwin? I'm Sandy Clare, Jack's mother. Do you remember? The two of you used to play in my yard and swim in the pool together. I work here in the County jail. I heard that you were here."

The name of Jack Clare sounded familiar, and the two of them did play together in grammar school. His remembrances came back. Yes! He did remember that Jack's mother worked in the jail, but was this really the jail? Why did she come to see him? Were they trying to get on his good side? Did she owe them a favor? Edwin was more confused than ever. He just stood and looked.

"How did you get the mark on your neck?" she asked.

"I tried to cut my throat."

"I'll get a nurse to take a look at it. I'm hoping the best for you."

And she left.

Sometime later a nurse did come to Edwin's cell to take a look at the cut. She looked at it, decided that it was only minor, and took no action other than to write in her chart that Edwin was a danger to himself.

Lunch arrived: two boiled hot dogs with slices of bread and something to drink. Edwin took a bite, then flushed it all down the toilet. He had been told that the food was poisoned. No bad effects resulted, though, from the mouthful he had eaten.

More time passed. Two guards came to his cell with handcuffs and an orange jumpsuit. One spoke.

"Put this on. The judge wants to see you."

So Edwin put the jumpsuit on. Then one guard put the cuffs on him, and they all walked over to the crowded courtroom where he was instructed to stand by the wall.

Bart Sanders made his way to Edwin's side and also instructed him.

"Let me talk. Don't say anything unless the judge asks you directly. Is that clear?"

"Yes."

In a few minutes his case was called.

"State versus Potter. Is Mr. Potter here?"

"Yes, Your Honor," answered Mr. Sanders.

"You are counsel for the defendant, Mr. Sanders?"

"Yes, Your Honor."

"You are prosecutor, Ms. Bailey?"

"Yes, Your Honor."

"What are the charges, Prosecutor?"

"At present two counts each of atrocious assault and battery with a weapon, Your Honor. I wish to point out at this time that the victims are currently in critical care at Saint Mark's Hospital. These charges may change pending any changes in their medical conditions."

"Mr. Sanders."

"I am requesting psychiatric observation for my client, Your Honor. He does not seem to understand the gravity of his situation at the present time. A medical note from the nurse at the County jail indicates that Mr. Potter is a danger to himself as well as to others. Also, according to the records available to us, Your Honor, Mr. Potter has no prior criminal history."

"Results of the urine test, Prosecutor?"

"Negative, Your Honor. No drug usage found."

The judge considered for a moment the arguments that he had just heard.

"All right. Effective immediately, Mr. Potter is to be sent to the maximum-security facility at State Psychiatric Hospital for observation for a period of thirty days. I will expect a report from the treating doctor at that time stating his findings and Mr. Potter's prognosis."

"Next case!"

Chapter 3: Daniel Aaron, Esq.

By the time Derek Potter got home from the police station that night his wife Ellen was an emotional wreck. She was still weeping when he entered the house.

"How is he?" she asked.

"Not good. He doesn't seem to know where he is."

"What happened?"

"The police from the County came and picked him up and brought him over to the jail. They didn't say what happens next."

There was silence, then suddenly an eruption.

"This is all your fault!" Ellen shouted.

"My fault? Why is this my fault?" Derek asked defensively.

"You really don't know, do you?"

"No, Ellen, I really don't know." Sarcasm began to creep into his voice. "Tell me why this is my fault."

"Because of your old man! That's why! Your old man was a wacko of all wackos!"

The argument reached a crescendo.

"Forget it, Ellen! Just forget it!"

The neighbors could hear them now.

"And forget Edwin, too, I suppose!"

"That's right! We'll forget him too!"

"He's our son, Derek! We can't just abandon him!"

"Why not? – "

"Why not? Are you out of your mind?"

"This is no little thing, Ellen! He's scarred for life! It will be nothing but hardship for us *and* for him! My old man was a wacko, and we had to live with that hell! My two cousins in the nursing home aren't thinking right either! I promised my aunt that I would take care of them when she died. Now this!"

"I don't know if I can do this, Derek! You're not the only one involved in this. How are we going to get through this?"

"I don't know, Ellen! We'll just have to do like we did before!"

Then an ugly, stormy silence filled the house.

Cautiously, Sasha – Edwin's sister younger by a few years – entered the room.

"What's all the yelling for?"

Derek and Ellen looked at each other. Ellen spoke.

"We have bad news about your brother."

"Why? What happened?"

"Amy and Denny are in critical care at Saint Mark's. Edwin says he did it. The police came and got him a short while ago."

Sasha stood quietly for a moment, and then broke into tears.

Eventually Derek said, "I'll call the attorney in the morning to see if he can recommend anybody."

* * *

This morning Edwin had stood before the Judge who sent him to State Psychiatric Hospital. That afternoon Derek and Ellen Potter seated themselves in front of the enormous wooden desk, across from the trial attorney. Surrounding all of them were shelf upon shelf of books of law, the culmination of years of humanity's search for the perfect society: one that is fair to all in all matters of human behavior with the goal to achieve a well-ordered society regulated by the Rule of Law.

Daniel Aaron, the attorney, was reviewing one of those tomes. The tip of his index finger was bent from the many years of running down the open page in the search for a paragraph written in his client's behalf. His white hair was thin over the top, and he wore a tweed suit, an anachronism from a younger day.

Mr. Aaron put the book aside.

"Mr. Aaron," began Derek, "our family attorney, Alex Francesco, recommended you to us."

Mr. Aaron shook his head in affirmation and spoke slowly and deliberately.

"Mr. Francesco called me this morning, and I agreed to see you today – posthaste. Time is of the essence."

"We don't even know where our son is at this point," said Ellen. "We think he's at the County jail."

"All right, Mr. and Mrs. Potter," said Mr. Aaron, slowly. "I'll check into that. In the meantime, I'm going to have to ask you some questions. Some of them may be painful."

"We'll cooperate any way we can."

"All right, let's begin. So that when I call the jail, what is your son's first name?"

"Edwin," said Derek.

"How old is he?"

"He's about twenty-four, twenty-five."

"How far did he go in school?"

"He graduated from a very good school a few years ago with a bachelor's degree in electrical engineering."

"He graduated with honor," added Ellen.

"That may be of interest to the judge," said Mr. Aaron, raising his gnarled index finger. "Now I have to ask you some very difficult questions. Was there any drug abuse – that you are aware of?"

"No," said Derek.

"Did you see him regularly?"

"I don't know what you mean by 'regularly.'"

"Did you see him on weekends, at special events like birthdays, holidays or some such other – ?"

"Mostly birthdays and holidays."

"That's good. Was there any alcohol abuse – that you are aware of?"

"No."

"Has he ever been in trouble with the law before?"

"No."

"Now, Mr. Francesco told me that Edwin is married. Did he and his wife have any children?"

"Yes. One. His name is Denny."

"How old is he?"

"Ellen, how old is Denny?"

"About two-and-a-half."

"Was he involved in the recent incident?"

"Yes," said Ellen. "He's in the hospital along with his mother. They're both in critical care."

There was an uncomfortable pause.

"Were they all living together under one roof at the time of the incident?"

"Yes."

"How would you describe Edwin's social behavior?"

"He's a loner. He's been that way for as long as we can remember."

"All right. Tell me, then, as well as you can, what you remember happening the night of the incident."

And so they told their story. The interview went on for about an hour, Mr. Aaron gleaning whatever information he could from Edwin's parents.

And then it was over.

"At this time our course of action is to have Edwin interviewed by a psychiatrist who will testify on his behalf at the trial – should it come to that. I have someone in mind who I will call as soon as you leave – a Doctor Desmond Edmonds. I assure you: He is very good."

"All right, then, if you think that's what we should do," said Derek. "My wife and I will leave you to do what you have to do. Thank you very much."

They left.

"Rose?" Mr. Aaron called out to his secretary. "Get me the number of a Doctor Desmond Edmonds over at Addison Memorial."

"Yes, Daniel."

Then to himself he added, "Then all we can do is wait."

Chapter 4: Father Daley and Dr. Desmond Edmonds

Edwin was looking at patterns change on the wall of his bare cell at State Psychiatric Hospital. Yesterday Edwin appeared before the judge. Evening passed. Two more meals on plastic trays again today. Now it was afternoon.

There are no patterns, Edwin. There are just green blocks with gray mortar in the joints.

But Edwin saw them.

"He is a genius!" he remembered being told.

With every new pattern or design he would remember a co-worker encouraging him onward, answering his every question, fulfilling every apparent prophecy – leading him down the path to ultimate futility and confusion.

"How do they know?" he argued with himself. "How do they know with complete accuracy what is coming? How do they read my mind now while they're in the past? The future hadn't happened yet!"

"Even the questions he asks – pure genius!"

Edwin was embarrassed.

"Do well in school, and don't think you're so smart. There are plenty of people in this world who are smarter than you," was what he was told. So he did well. Always on the Honor Roll or the Dean's List, but he was never encouraged to think for himself or to express his own opinion.

Where was this place? What was this place? It was a long drive – maybe two hours at police speeds – from the County jail, but he had made it. Initially he hadn't been certain that he would. Prior to their leaving he had watched the police officers load their guns, and Edwin believed that they would stop somewhere along the route and shoot him dead. As there was no escape, he had resolved himself to his fate.

And then they had driven up to this old, abandoned concrete fortress with bars and gates at every turn. Had they acquired it for purposes like Edwin's? Was it just for him that they went through this? How big was this project? How important was Edwin? Now that he was here, were they now going to abandon him and let him die if he did not perform? Was this a plot to make him bring the project to a successful completion? There would be no escape from his cell. And no one would know that he was there.

A mouse running by stopped to peek into his cell and sniff. Then it continued on its way. In a minute there was the voice of an old man echoing from somewhere nearby.

"Hey! There's a mouse in my room!"

There was silence.

"Hey!" the voice repeated. "There's a mouse in my room!"

"Don't worry about it," said a tired voice in reply.

"If I catch him I'm gonna eat him!"

"You gotta catch him first."

Edwin took this as a grim hint. Everyone here would be released, leaving him, and he would have to survive on the mice that ran past his cell. How many could he expect to do that? His memories only repeated his thoughts, praising him for his insights.

"Hey!" said the voice of the old man again. "There's water all over my room!"

"Where's it coming from?"

"Let me look...! It's coming from the pipes over my bed! It must be leaking from the toilet upstairs!"

There was another silence.

"Well, move your bed, and we'll see about moving you to a different room."

There was the sound of something moving next door to Edwin.

"I got water everywhere!"

"That's all that we can do for you right now. Move it to a dry spot."

"I got water everywhere! Look for yourself!"

A thin, gray-haired black man in a guard uniform – a white shirt, dark pants, and carrying a whistle and a two-way radio – came and stood in front of Edwin's cell.

"Potter?"

"Yes."

"Drink this," he said, placing a paper cup onto the iron crossbar.

Edwin picked up the cup and sniffed at it.

"Just drink the shit or I'll write you up!" shouted the guard.

Edwin did as he was told, abandoning his own sense of self-preservation.

The guard took back the empty cup and said, "You got a visitor." Then without turning he shouted, "Open six!"

With a noise and a clatter, the gate to Edwin's cell opened. Edwin did not move.

"Come out."

"Look at the water in here!" cried the old man.

The guard ignored him as Edwin exited his cell and was led by the guard to the iron gate at the end of the row where there was another guard who had opened the gate. They passed him and went down the stairs and through a few more gates before Edwin was ushered into what would be best described as similar to a living room. There was wood trim, a plain rug on the floor, and plain but comfortable furniture where a priest was standing. Edwin recognized him as Father

Shawn Daley who he knew from the Roman Catholic church that he and his family attended. Father Shawn sat as the guard moved to the side to leave them alone.

"I saw what happened in the papers, and I came down to see if you're all right. I called your parents, and they told me that you are here."

Edwin said nothing. Father Shawn went on.

"In some ways you are a model for some couples in the parish who have bad marriages. They want to work now to make them better. Can you tell me what happened?"

Edwin related his story briefly.

"Do you know what you did?"

"I saved them," said Edwin and then hung his head in grief.

Father Shawn placed his hand onto Edwin's head and gave him absolution, then nodded to the guard that he was finished and left.

The guard whispered a few words with Father Shawn, then announced quietly, "Potter. Doctor wants to see you now. Come this way."

The guard ushered Edwin down the hall to a stark, block-walled room. In it were a table and two wooden chairs. A bald-headed man wearing a brown suit was already seated and chewing on a cigar as Edwin took a seat. He gave Edwin a long look. On the table before him was a tired, brown attaché case that he opened briefly, took out a folder, and closed quickly. Instead of placing the case on the floor, he left it on the table before him as though it were a valuable commodity. The guard closed the door heavily behind him and waited outside. In the meantime, the man opened his folder, set it on the case, and began the interview. To Edwin he looked like the devil. It made him nervous.

"I'm Doctor Desmond Edmonds," the man said, taking the cigar from his mouth. "What's your name?"

"Edwin Potter."

Doctor Edmonds checked his papers to see what notes had already been written into the chart. Satisfied, he continued.

"How old are you?"

"Twenty-five."

"What are you here for?"

Edwin clenched his teeth. They were testing him. The doctor who looked like the devil was their advocate. They wanted to see if Edwin would expose them. Could Edwin be trusted? Tell the truth!

Edwin replied with difficulty, "I killed my wife and son."

Doctor Edmonds paused, then made another note.

"Are your parents still alive?"

"Yes."

"Both of them?"

"Yes."

"How far did you go in school?"

"I have a bachelor's degree with honor in electrical engineering."

"When did you graduate?"

"Three years ago."

Doctor Edmonds made a note.

"Do you use drugs?

"Aspirin."

"Do you use illegal drugs?"

"No."

"Do you drink alcohol?"

"Maybe a glass of wine with dinner."

"OK... Have you ever been hospitalized before?"

Is that what this was?

"No."

"Is there any history of mental illness in your family?"

"My grandfather was diagnosed with schizophrenia with homicidal tendencies."

"Your grandfather?"

"Yes."

"Which side of the family?'

"My father's side. He chased my father with a knife."

There was silence as the doctor listened carefully.

"Is he still alive?"

"No. He died when I was very young."

A thoughtful pause.

"Anyone else with a history?"

"No."

"Are you on any medication?"

"No."

Doctor Edmonds looked at one of the pages in his folder.

"The hospital records show that you're on Thorazine."

Edwin flustered.

"I don't know. They gave me a cup of something. I don't know what it was."

The doctor made a face.

"Do you know what ward you're on?"

"They didn't tell me."

"You're on ward seven. That's as far down as you can go in our society. Even prison is a step up."

With that disclosed, the doctor continued.

"Do you have any siblings?"

"I have one sister."

"Has she ever been treated for mental illness?"

"No."

"Now tell me: What happened the other night that brought you here?"

Edwin's heart raced. What could he say? How could he continue with this and not expose them? They already knew what happened. The fear of death filled Edwin again, but it didn't matter. His wife and child were dead. This doctor couldn't hurt them.

"I thought they were going to force me to complete a doomed project --."

"Doomed?"

"Yes."

"How were they going to force you?"

"They were going to kidnap my wife and son and torture them to make me perform."

The doctor thought for a moment.

"Who are 'they'?"

Edwin froze. He had given them away! "Oh, my God! Oh, my God!" he thought.

Getting no response, Doctor Edmonds continued.

"They – whoever 'they' are – were going to kidnap your wife and son. So how does that tie in with your actions?"

"I was saving them from a fate worse than death."

The doctor's jaw slackened as he heard this.

"Do you have any hallucinations? No – let me ask this: Have you ever seen anything unusual like people on fire or – space aliens for example?"

"I remember seeing one woman standing alone out in the middle of a parking lot at one time. I thought to myself, 'What is this woman doing?' That's the only thing that I can remember."

"What was so unusual about that?"

"I was just wondering why she was standing out there so obviously alone."

The doctor thought about that then made a note.

"Was there any argument leading up to your action at home?"

"No."

"Overall, have you ever made any violent outbursts?"

"No."

"Have you ever just hauled off and smacked somebody?"

"No."

"Has anyone in your family ever had a violent outburst?"

"No."

"Do you know what happened to you?"

Edwin was confused now. What had happened to him? Nothing had happened to him other than that they were pursuing him, and he got caught. He flustered again but said nothing of value.

Doctor Edmonds brought the interview to an end, packed his briefcase as quickly as he had unpacked it before and stood up. The interview had taken about an hour.

"I'll submit the report to your attorney by tomorrow afternoon," the doctor said. "I hope you get better soon."

With that the door opened, and the guard led Edwin back to his cell.

Time passed. Another tray.

In his cell Edwin thought about what he had seen. He had seen the devil and answered all of his questions. And Edwin had thought, "Oh, my God!" Who was his God? Shouldn't he have called upon the name of the Lord and cast the devil out? Why didn't he? Again he had failed to take action just as he had failed to take action with the prostitutes. What would his evangelical friends say about that after all of their years of teaching him the Ways of The Lord? The image grew more intense. Was he a demon? Had he just sold his soul to the devil? Was he deceived? Had he deceived himself for all of his life? Maybe the devil was taking orders from him. Who was he, Edwin, then?

Edwin began to feel the demons that possessed him rise up in him. He looked at his arms and saw scales begin to form.

"Cast them out! Cast them out! Call upon the name of Jesus and cast them out!"

His voice became a deep-throated roar that rose and soared. He screamed like a demon as he called upon the name of the Lord. He felt them! He felt the demons!

"Oh, Jesus, save me!"

But to no avail. Why wasn't it working?

And he roared again and again, calling in a terrified, futile effort upon the name of Jesus for half of the night until he fell in exhaustion.

Chapter 5: Tangentially Speaking

The young and lovely TV news reporter put the microphone up to her mouth and began to speak.

"Behind me is the home where the stillness of this quiet part of town was broken yesterday. A man identified as Edwin Potter attacked his own family – his wife and his infant son – by hitting them both over the head with an iron bar and then running to the home of his parents where the police arrested him.

"We approached both his neighbors and his parents. None of them had any comment. I have here with me County Prosecutor Georgia Bailey. Prosecutor, what is your comment on this case?"

"Clearly this is a heinous crime. Edwin Potter is a threat to our society and in order to protect the people of our society must never be allowed to be free again. We intend to prosecute to the fullest extent of the law."

"We have reports, Prosecutor, that the condition of one of the victims is worsening. What would you do if the worst should occur?"

"We would pursue the death penalty."

"Thank you, Prosecutor."

The camera closed in on the reporter.

"That was County Prosecutor Georgia Bailey commenting on the recent violence here. Remember: We report. You decide. Back to you in the studio."

* * *

Assemblyman Glenn Keenan turned off the TV news and the pretty young woman with it.

"I hope he dies – unloved and unmourned. The sooner the better," he said. "These miscreants are eating up the State budget."

"I'm sure that you'll think of something," said his wife. "You always do."

"What was that?"

"Nothing."

With a moment's thought, Keenan ignored his wife's remark and got up to look out the window at his empty in-ground pool in the back yard. He was thinking about something.

"Where are the neighbors?" he asked. "I haven't seen them for the past few days."

"They're on vacation. They won't be back until the end of the week."

"Oh," he said, still in thought and looking at the pool. "I'm going outside."

Without further discussion he left the house and went into the garage to find a long garden hose. He succeeded and came out and put one end into the empty swimming pool. Then he brought the remainder over to the fence and threw it into the neighbor's yard. He went around the fence to the gate, opened it, then went over to the hose to pick it up. With a few more steps he brought the end over to the faucet, attached the hose, and turned on the water.

* * *

Sasha was seated at her parents' kitchen table with her fiancé Larry Cisco. She was distraught.

"I don't know what we should do," she said. "Should we get married or shouldn't we?"

"I say yes."

"You don't understand, Larry. I have people calling me on the phone and telling me 'I didn't know that your brother is a murderer.' I can't handle it. And what about our children? Are they going to grow up normal? These things are genetic: my grandfather had it, now my brother. And now the Prosecutor wants to kill him."

She burst into tears. Larry could only sit in silence and wait it out. He took her hand.

"Is this the kind of life that we want? That we'll have to live with?" she continued.

He thought for a moment.

"Well, what would you do if we don't get married? Live at home with your parents? Live in a convent? And maybe someday you'll get tired of that and find someone else to marry – much to my disappointment – only to come full circle.

"The time is now, Sasha. Life is filled with the unknown, and we will have to face those things as they come. I love you, and I am willing to make the sacrifices necessary to take care of you and our children as well as any of the problems that we all might have – come hell or high water. What do you say?"

"You make sense, but I don't know what to say... I need to be alone for a while."

Chapter 6: The Book of Tears

     It was Sunday, a rainy day at the end of July. One and a half weeks had passed since the incident, and there was no improvement in Edwin's thinking. There were several psychiatrists who had come to interview him. Same questions. They were all the same.

     "Potter!" called the guard down ward seven. "Doctor says you can go to population."

     Edwin broke into a sweat. Population was where they were going to corner him and kill him.

     A guard stood in front of Edwin's cell as the gate opened.

     "Let's go, Potter. We're going to the Day Room."

     Edwin pleaded as he did at the jail, this time not reaching out to anger the guard, "Please don't put me in population! They'll kill me!"

     "Nobody's going to kill you. Let's go."

     Edwin, having no better argument, stepped acquiescently out of his cell.

     "Where are my glasses?"

     "We got your glasses. Don't worry about them."

Down the hall he walked with the guard, and together they passed the guard station. Again more stairs with iron gates and eventually a hallway where sounds – the cacophony of radios and a television and loud talking with an occasional shout – were coming from the other end. Another guard unlocked the gate to the Day Room, and Edwin Potter stepped into a world of madness.

A blue haze of smoke was the first thing that hit him followed by the stench of stale urine and unwashed bodies. There were about seventy men. Most of them were wearing blue jeans. Others wore chinos. Some of the pants were torn or did not fit right. Edwin was still wearing the jeans and shirt he wore when he was arrested. Some men did not have a shirt to wear or, in the case of the blacks, they had torn tee shirts to make do-rags that they wore on their heads. Some had no shoes. The floors and walls of this snake pit were filthy. One of the two toilets – installed directly in the Day Room with no front doors – was cracked, and the water was running into a drain in the center of the floor.

"Is this what they will provide? Is this my future?" wondered Edwin.

These were among the most dangerous men in society. Many of these men were smoking, seated on the few park benches and picnic tables that were brought in to provide seating. One man sat on a bench and smoked his cigarette, rocking back and forth in agitation until he finally got up and walked stiffly around the perimeter of the room. He swung one hand widely and held his coffin nail to his lips with the other, not caring whether he walked in the water or not. Another man was also pacing the perimeter of the room and talking to himself in complete gibberish. Suddenly he just smacked a person in the head as he went by. And just as suddenly there was a commotion started by the man who was hit. He jumped up, and the culprit – gangly and of short stature – got into a boxing stance, dancing around. A few guards moved in slowly so as not to precipitate a fight or get caught in one.

"What happened?" one of them asked.

"Slick hit me!"

"Slick? Slick hit you?"

"Yeah!"

"What he hit you for?"

"How the fuck should I know?"

"Well, just keep out of his way next time."

One guard, Rex Walker, was standing arrogantly and surveying the room. He spoke loudly for all to hear.

"All these mother-fuckers belong in prison on Death Row! Every single one of them! They don't bring no good to nobody! They ain't good for shit! They just eat up taxes that should be used somewhere else than some hellhole like this! Even this is too good for them!"

Edwin took those words into account and then saw an open space at one of the benches. He went and sat down, still taking everything in, still wondering what their plan was. Across the room from Edwin was a black man, a real troublemaker in Edwin's distorted reasoning.

"Edwin Potter!" shouted a high-pitched voice.

It had come from one of the guards near the gate. Edwin did not know what to do. Could this be the moment of execution?

"Edwin Potter!" the guard called again.

Edwin got up and went to him, identifying himself. The guard looked at him, sizing him up.

"You got a visit. Go with Green. Willie Green!" he called.

Green, standing right nearby, gave a big smile.

"You got a visit! All right! What's your name?"

"Edwin Potter."

"OK, Edwin! Let's go!"

And away through the fortress they went until they reached a small room with about five windows, each with a chair and a phone. Edwin could see some people on the other side of one window.

"Have a seat there," said Green, indicating the window with the people. "I'll be outside."

Green stepped out. There was no door to close.

Edwin turned to the window, took his seat, and picked up the phone. Suddenly he recognized Deangelo and Olivia Cuccinelli. He and Amy knew them from the Assembly of God where they attended church during Edwin's college days. Olivia was the pastor's daughter. They were happy people, but today they looked very somber. Deangelo did all of the talking.

"We can't stay long. I didn't realize how long it takes to get here."

They talked small talk. They talked about the Bible. They did not talk about the incident. Edwin sat in silence as he usually did, answering only when asked.

"Is Pastor coming?" asked Edwin, finally, confused as ever. Were they really Deangelo and Olivia? Did these two owe them a favor as well? The prophecies were coming true. He remembered his co-workers telling him that they would come for a visit.

"He said he's busy. He was against our coming, so this is the last time that we will see each other. We came to say good-bye. God be with you."

Edwin did not understand. He watched silently as both of them got up and walked out of his life forever, down the corridor never to be seen again.

"That's a shame, Ed," said Willie Green, returning. "You really get to know who your friends are." He stepped out for a moment. Edwin could hear him talking with someone.

"Hold on!" said Green, coming back into the visit room. "There's someone else for you! Just stay right there!"

Someone for him? A friend? Who could it be?

Two people approached the window. As they sat down he recognized them as his parents. Something looked wrong, though.

"Hi, Ed. We're sorry that we couldn't make it here last Sunday. We called the hospital to ask them about visiting hours, and they said to wait another week because you were under observation. So that's that. We have your keys and your wallet. They gave them to us when we got here. So now we can lock the house. Where are your glasses?"

Almost as though on cue, Green came into the room with a pair of glasses and a brown paper shopping bag of items. He gave them to Edwin with a quiet word.

"Ed," said Ellen Potter, "we have bad news... Amy died on Thursday."

Edwin was confused. Amy had died on that night, but he couldn't tell her because that would reveal their plot. What should he say?

"I-I. She would have only been a vegetable any other way."

His parents froze. After a moment his mother said, "I guess you're right," and turned away to cry.

"When I get out," said Edwin, "I need to find someone to marry again."

"Don't rush it, Ed. You need to stay in there for at least a little while longer," said his mother.

"Why?" Edwin asked himself. Why do they keep him locked up like this? Why couldn't he walk freely like a normal person? Wasn't he just as normal as everyone else?

His father spoke up slowly and in control. "Ed, we brought some things. Some clothes. Some fruit. We brought you a book and a radio. Now you can keep yourself busy. What do they have you do all day?"

"Nothing."

"No therapies? No groups? No activities?"

"No. They just put me into population."

"What's population?"

"It's where they put everybody."

"Well, that explains that," said Ellen bravely.

Edwin was silent. After a brief moment his mother spoke.

"Ed, I didn't tell you about Denny. He's getting better. He's a fighter that little guy. The doctors are saying that there is a chance that he might pull through... Also, we didn't have a chance to tell you: We had to hire an attorney. His name is Daniel Aaron. He recommended that your father and I adopt Denny so that there won't be any custody disagreements with your in-laws about him in the future – if it ever comes to that. We will have to go to Court. Are you willing to agree to that?"

Edwin was confused. His son lived and was in danger. And there was no way to protect him. What could he do?

"OK," he said weakly.

"OK," Ellen continued. "We'll tell the lawyer... Did a psychiatrist come to see you?"

Edwin was still confused. What was real? Who were all of these people? Were they really his parents? His parents were replaced by space aliens when he was very young. He remembered vividly. That explained so many things. So who were these "psychiatrists"?

"A few," he answered.

"How many is 'a few'?" asked Derek?

"Three."

"Let's figure this out now... Aaron said that he sent two... The third one must have been from the prosecutor. Anybody else?"

"No."

"Have you seen the hospital psychiatrist?

"Which one is he?"

Derek paused.

"That's a good question," he said. "I guess you don't know."

And that was about it. From there this conversation, too, wound down to small talk. After an hour Derek and Ellen called it time to go and promised him that they would be back the following week.

Green came in and reminded Edwin to take his bag with him back to population. And so they went back to the Day Room as they had come.

When they arrived, Edwin took the same seat that he had when he left. And there, across the room, was the same black that had caught his attention earlier.

"You must fight him!" his memories told him.

"No! Why should I fight him?"

"You must fight him! He needs to be put in his place!"

"I've never been in a fight in my life! What purpose does it have?"

"You must fight him!"

Edwin began to shake as his memories began to win. He worked himself up, then stood up and strode quickly over to the man, leaving his bag on the table.

"OK! Let's go! I'm gonna take care of you!" He put up his fists.

The black man took the challenge and jumped up to his fighting position. They danced around each other. Then the black man swung out with a hard left and caught Edwin in the jaw. Edwin staggered, then fell heavily to the floor as the victor stood over him. It had taken less than thirty seconds.

The guards moved in and moved the man away from Edwin. One of them took a look inside Edwin's mouth. In the meantime, another patient was going through Edwin's bag. Green told him to stay away, but the man pulled out a pair of socks and an orange and swore at him before he moved away. Green picked up the bag as the men were called out of the Day Room and back to their cells. It was the end of the day.

The guard who had looked inside Edwin's mouth decided that Edwin needed medical attention and got on his radio to call the control center and arrange for a dentist to look at him. That done, Green bade Edwin to follow him, and they walked to a very bare examining room. Soon the dentist arrived and took a look inside Edwin's mouth.

"You did a fine job of holding onto your teeth," he commented, still looking. "We'll have to get him over to surgery as soon as we can," was the final remark, and he made a note in Edwin's chart.

So Edwin was left in the examining room with Green. A guard supervisor poked his head in the door for a quick word with Green about overtime. Green declined.

"OK. I'll find somebody to relieve you... A car is on its way to take you over to the surgical unit." His radio came on telling him that the car was outside. He relayed the message to Green.

So they put a leather belt with handcuffs on it onto Edwin, then two guards led him to the waiting car where he got in, then Green and the other guard, and they drove the one hundred yards to the surgical unit where they had a room waiting. In the room they removed the cuffs and belt and told him to get into the bed where they cuffed him to the side rail.

The other guard left leaving Green to pull up a chair for watch duty. There they waited.

After a short while a young nurse came in and wanted to talk, excited about the opportunity to see someone from the maximum-security facility.

"She is meant for you," Edwin's memories told him.

"I realize your jaw is broken," said the nurse, "so I'll just ask you yes or no questions, and you can nod your head. OK?"

Edwin shook his head yes. So she asked him some questions. Did he like sports? He gestured with open hands. Baseball? No. Basketball? No. Football? Ah, yes. Did he have a job before he came to the hospital? Yes.

"Engineer," he said to shorten the questioning.

She did not ask him why he was in the hospital or what was happening to him. She did not ask him about family or children. Then two medical personnel came into the room to prep him for surgery. The young nurse left, never to be seen again.

Chapter 7: A New Way of Life

Several days had passed since Edwin had had his jaw broken and then wired in the hospital. If he talked, it could be done only through his clenched teeth. He was on a liquid diet until the wires were removed. He had also been moved to a new ward: ward two. It looked like ward seven.

The thing that had worried him most when he returned to population was running into the black man again and having to run with his tail between his legs. No more. He was not going to live the life of a coward. Let them kill him. When he saw the black man again, he glared at him despite his wired mouth and saw fear in the man as he went by. It didn't matter. In a few days the man had been sent back to prison; there was nothing wrong with him.

At this time Edwin was sitting at one of the wooden picnic tables in the dining hall waiting for the hospital psychiatrist. The dining hall was where Edwin ate with everyone else now that he had been moved to the new ward. No more trays under the iron gate although there were still gates. The floor and tables were clean, but there was the pervasive smell of a dirty, wet mop. The humidity only made it worse. There was no air conditioning here in the dining hall or anywhere else. And there was always a guard nearby.

Suddenly an energetic old man with white hair came into the room carrying a number of folders. He was dressed like he had been out on safari and took a seat across from Edwin at the table. Edwin's prophetic memories from the past started up at the sight. The doctor was here to investigate him and show him that they were not going to play with him. They wanted the project done successfully and that fight was just a taste of what they would do to him if he did not cooperate. He argued with his memories comprised of his co-workers, his family, his friends, people he knew from the past. All of them were in on it.

"Mr. Potter?"

"Yes?" he said through his clenched teeth.

"I'm Doctor Rolf Brinkerhoff. I am your treating psychiatrist," he said, waiting to see Edwin's response. Seeing none, he continued, "I heard that you got into a fight earlier this week?"

"Yes."

"What happened?"

Edwin hesitated.

"I said the wrong thing."

The doctor thought about it for a moment, then continued.

"What county are you from?"

"Midland."

"Midland! Oh, that's a long ride! But if I have to I guess that I'll have to make it... Tell me, Mr. Potter, what happened that night a few weeks ago?"

They were testing him again, but so far, for the most part, there had been no retaliation for telling his story.

"My employer was going to kidnap my wife and son and hold them as hostages in order to make me complete a major project successfully."

"And how does that affect you?"

"They were going to torture them if I did not comply."

"I don't understand. What made you take your actions?"

"I was saving them from a fate worse than death."

A pause. Always a pause. What were they thinking?

"Was there an argument?"

"No."

Another pause.

"Have you talked with your attorney?"

"I don't have an attorney."

"Do you have family?"

"Yes."

"I will talk with them. In the meantime, I want you to meet with a psychology intern – today. She will give you some tests, and we will go from there."

"OK."

"Finally, I am going to take you off of the Thorazine and see how you react. Any comments?

"No."

With that Doctor Brinkerhoff got up and left. The guard motioned to Edwin to remain seated. A few minutes passed before a young woman entered the dining hall, and, like the doctor, took a seat at the picnic table across from Edwin.

"I'm Michelle Baker. How are you today?"

"Fine."

"OK, I would like to give you some tests that the Doctor just told you about. Do you mind?"

"No."

"Before that, though, is there anything that you would like to tell me?"

"No."

"All right. I would also like to make arrangements for getting you into art therapy. Would you be willing to do that?"

"OK."

"Good. I'll speak with the therapist, and she can schedule an interview."

"She is for you," said his memories. Edwin argued back in his mind with them. They responded. How do they do that? How do they know?

"OK," Edwin said to Ms. Baker.

"OK. First I want to get some background information."

She pulled out a paper tablet. Edwin continued to argue with himself.

"How old are you?"

Edwin began to get angry.

"Twenty-five," he seethed through his wired teeth.

"Are your parents still living?"

"Yes," he seethed.

"Do you use drugs?"

Edwin showed his anger.

"Don't you people talk to each other?"

Edwin's outburst caught the guard's attention.

"I've been answering these questions for weeks, and you're all still asking me the same ones over and over!"

Ms. Baker held back.

"Well, maybe we can do this part later…"

Edwin calmed down, his mind still actively misinterpreting everything.

"I know that it's difficult, but I want to ask about the incident at your home several weeks ago. Why didn't you ask for help?"

"Help with what?"

Ms. Baker thought for a moment.

"Don't you ever ask for help?" she asked.

"What kind of help?"

"Psychological help."

"N-no," he said, not knowing where the discussion was going.

"Why is that?"

More flustering.

"It's a sign of weakness."

Ms. Baker looked at him some more, and then went on, "All right. I'd like to give you those tests. One of them is an IQ test. Have you ever been given an IQ test before?"

"No."

"OK. The IQ test will have to be done on another day. To do all of these tests in one day will not be possible."

And so the personality tests began. When they were finished about an hour later, Edwin was brought back to population. There he just looked for a seat where he could bide his time until they were all called to go back upstairs to their cells. One had to be careful of which seat he chose. Some of them were "owned".

"Here! Sit here!" said someone behind him. Edwin turned around and saw an older man. He had tousled blonde hair and a mustache. Crow's feet were beginning to establish themselves at the corners of his eyes, and he had a few books stacked in front of him as well as a denim jacket that lay over them. The apparent speaker held out his hand in a gesture to indicate the empty seat opposite him at the table.

"Does anyone sit there?"

"Don't worry about it. He's an idiot. Take the seat."

So Edwin seated himself. For a few moments there was a silence as both of them wondered who should speak first – and what information to divulge. Then the speaker decided to take the initiative.

"I saw you for the past few days or so. You're new here. What's your name?"

"Edwin Potter."

"Well, glad to meet you, Ed," he said and squinted at him.

More silence as they waited each other out.

"What are you here for?" the man asked.

Edwin thought for a moment.

"I don't want to talk about it."

"All right," replied the other. "Most people here don't... My name is Frank Kirkland since you didn't ask."

They shook hands.

As they were warming up, another man came and stood near to them.

"Ah! Dom Sanchez!" said Frank. "He got his name from the designer tag on the inside of his shirt... Dom, this is Edwin Potter."

"I see him. Don't make fun of my name! What's he doing in my seat?"

"Looks to me like he's sitting there. So what about it?"

Edwin began to worry about being caught in another fight and getting hit again in the jaw.

"I don't want people to sit where I sit."

"What are you going to do about it?"

"I-I."

And Dom strode away to the next room. Suddenly there was the sound of a guard's whistle, and all the guards ran to it. As Edwin and Frank watched, they saw the guards with Dom in a hold as they walked him back to lock-up on ward seven.

And Frank sighed in wearied disgust.

"He has poor conflict resolution skills."

And both of them watched after him as he was taken down the hall.

Edwin caught sight of an old man sitting motionless by himself over in a corner.

"Who is that?"

Frank looked in the direction of Edwin's gesture.

"That's Roger Breakstone. Sad story. He is a war hero. Many years ago he lost control, took a rifle, and shot and killed eleven people. They'll never let him out. They keep him all doped up on medication. Only his mother comes to see him."

Suddenly a balding man wearing an army jacket rushed over and seated himself into a nearby, newly vacated chair.

"I'm going to kill that motherfucker!" he declared.

"Kill who?" asked Frank. "As if I didn't know...."

"Jacob Schmidt, asshole! Director of this building!"

"And why is that, Paul Gregory?"

"Because he doesn't know if I'm crazy or not!"

"Well, are you crazy?"

"I'm crazy as hell – and dangerous, too!"

"Well, just don't do anything that you'll come to regret..."

"Mind your own business, Kirkland, or I'll take care of you, too!"

Chapter 8: Loose Ends

"This is a hearing for the adoption of the infant Denny Potter. Enter your appearances for the record, please," said Judge Griffin, judge for the family court in Midland County.

"Alex Francesco, attorney for the parents of Edwin Potter."

"Linda Fitzgerald, attorney for Theresa Mann, mother of the deceased Amy Potter."

"We'll get to that," commented the judge. "I see that Barbara Dee is here as well. I take it that you are the social worker for this case?"

"Yes, Your Honor."

"What did you find in your investigation? Where is the child now?"

"Denny Potter is in the intensive care unit of Saint Mark's hospital here in town. I interviewed the treating doctor and staff, and they are of the medical opinion that the child will recover. How much is not yet clear. They expect to start rehabilitative therapy the day after tomorrow."

"Ms. Fitzgerald, you said that the mother – What is it?"

"Amy Potter."

"Amy Potter is deceased?"

"Yes, Your Honor. There was an incident at the home where her husband attacked her and their child with a weapon. Amy Potter died just recently – within the past two weeks."

"Mr. Francesco, where is the husband now, Edwin Potter?"

"He is in the maximum-security facility at State Psychiatric Hospital. His psychiatric diagnosis and prognosis are pending. We do not know if he will ever recover if he is found to be insane."

"Is the father in favor of this custody action?"

"We asked him Your Honor, and he is in favor."

The judge paused.

"Is this the only child of that marriage?"

"Yes, Your Honor."

"Ms. Dee, is there any history of criminal behavior anywhere in this case?"

"Aside from the current situation, no, Your Honor."

"Ms. Mann. Is your husband here today?"

"No. He died about two years ago from natural causes."

"Are you living with anyone?"

"No, Your Honor."

"How do you support yourself?" asked Judge Griffin.

"I work as a production supervisor in Dover City."

"What kind of business is that?"

"Embroidery."

"Full time?"

"Yes. I also receive survivor benefits from Social Security."

"So I guess that you are out of the house for most of the day for at least five days per week?"

"Yes, Your Honor."

Again there was a pause.

"How would you care for this child and provide him with the nurturing and the daily care that he would need, especially if he requires extra care because he is disabled?"

"It would be difficult, Your Honor."

"Mr. Potter, in what business are you employed?"

"I'm self-employed, Your Honor. Presently I run a commercial art business."

"How many people do you employ?"

"It's just me and my wife. We work out of our home."

"Do you have health insurance?"

"Yes, Your Honor."

"Mrs. Potter, let me ask you the same question that I asked Ms. Mann just a moment ago. Would you be able to provide the care and supervision that this child will need?"

"I raised my own two children under similar work conditions. Yes, Your Honor, I can care for Denny."

After a bit of thought, the judge made his decision.

"The Court awards the adoption of Denny Potter to Derek and Ellen Potter. Case dismissed."

***

So Edwin and his parents took their places at the visitation window that following Sunday.

"We received the Family Court decision to adopt Denny this past week," said Ellen Potter. "The alternatives were that, a foster home or an orphanage. Don't worry. We'll take good care of him."

Edwin remained silent. His memories spoke to him again. He remembered the faces, the voices, and the very words that each speaker used. He tried to remember more. It seemed so real. He argued the facts with himself. Deeper and deeper he would go only to exhaust himself.

"We have more good news. Sasha decided to marry Larry. The wedding will be in October. We didn't know whether to tell you or not. We didn't know how you would take it. Something else now: Your father bought a *How to Draw* book for you."

"To take your mind off of your problems," added Derek. "It shows you how to draw faces. Maybe someday when you get well you can come to work with me in the commercial art business. You may not be able to get a job anywhere else, but first you have to get well."

And Edwin wondered what he was talking about.

***

It was another lazy summer day for the patients at State hospital. Today they were let outside into the courtyard for some fresh air and some sunshine. There was some green grass and a gazebo with park benches where they could lie down and go to sleep. There were also high concrete walls with concertina wire to discourage their dreams of reaching freedom. If one looked hard enough he could also see the gun towers where men with guns and occasionally K-9 units were set to further discourage any ideas of leaving the psychiatric facility before the proper time.

Edwin was walking around the perimeter of the courtyard when he came upon a bearded man wearing a long cloak and a towel wrapped around his head like a turban who was talking loudly to no one.

"I am an imam! A teacher of the Word of God, the Koran! The Bible says that the fear of the Lord is the beginning of wisdom! The Koran says that he who blasphemes the name of The Prophet must die! I am here to carry out that mission!"

Edwin walked past him, but he was reminded of his Christian mission, his duty, which was to bring the Good News of Jesus Christ to those who would hear it.

Suddenly he spied someone. An olive man with short hair who was wearing little more than a tee shirt and jeans. He was wearing his shoes improperly so they flopped on his feet. And he was alone so that he and Edwin would not be disturbed.

"What's your name?"

"Stan."

"Have you heard the Good News of Jesus Christ?"

"No."

"Jesus came to save us from our sins and bring us to eternal life. Would you like that?"

"Yes."

So Edwin asked him to recite the formula with him to accept Jesus into his heart. Then he asked Stan if he would like to be baptized.

"Yes."

So Edwin saw a puddle of clear water over in the corner of the yard and led Stan to it. Then he cupped his hand and dribbled water onto Stan's head three times, invoking the names of the three Persons of the Holy Trinity.

Then it was over. Stan thanked Edwin and went on his way. Edwin stood and watched him go. Faith formation would have to wait for another day.

Edwin was called from this paradise and brought to the dining hall where he again met Michelle Baker.

"I have the results of the tests," she said. "On the IQ test you did very well. Your score was above average.

Edwin did not know what to ask.

"On the personality tests you are self-described as schizophrenic, paranoid type."

"How does this fit in with their plan to make me perform for them?" he wondered.

"Would you like to ask me anything?"

"I don't know what to ask."

"Well, let's just leave it at that then. You can speak with your therapist as these topics arise."

Chapter 9: Art Therapy

One month had passed. Frank Kirkland, Dom Sanchez, and Edwin Potter were seated about the picnic table in the dining hall and were listening to the art therapist, Susan. As was her wont she started her session with a discussion.

"Frank, why are you here?"

He thought for a moment and then responded sarcastically, "I'm here for the crime of mental illness! A crime punishable by death!"

"Some see it that way," she said. "What's your IQ?"

He shrugged, then responded, "High enough to get into The High-IQ Society."

"What's that?"

"An international high-IQ society."

"I... didn't expect that." Then she whispered to herself, "Don't encourage him."

"Why not?" asked Frank, overhearing.

"This type of therapy is for those who show some promise of recovery. Not everyone can be saved."

"So why doesn't that contradict what you just said? You have to encourage a person to get better or why bother?"

"I'll bring that up. But let's change the subject. Dom, how are you today?"

"I'm all right. I feel good. I feel strong."

"He thinks big and fat means big and strong!" Frank mocked.

"There he goes again!" said Dom holding out his hand to indicate Frank. "He always has something nasty to say! Now I don't feel so good! He's messing with my mind!"

"You need something else to think about."

"Think about what? I have nothing. I'm going nowhere."

"Think harder."

Susan asked Dom, "How far did you go in school?"

"Eighth grade. What do you need to know that for?"

"Maybe you should try to get your GED."

"Then you can be fat and educated," chided Frank.

"All right, all right" said Susan. "Frank, what are you thinking right now?"

"I saw Edwin baptizing Stan the other day."

"And?"

"I don't know his situation, but it seems... reckless... that someone would just give a Bible to someone else and expect everything to be well."

"Some do think that way."

"It's insane! More of the very thing that led to the problem is now supposed to fix it."

"Is that the answer?"

"What else is there? Abandon hope, all ye who enter here!" cried Frank.

Susan paused, and then asked Frank directly, "Is it easier to kill the second time?"

Frank winced and closed his eyes, seeming to keep the tears from coming.

"He was my father," he whispered.

"Were you on drugs?"

Pain began to show on Frank's face.

"I was supposed to ask...," she said.

"By whom?"

Susan said nothing, and then turned toward Edwin.

"I heard that Doctor Brinkerhoff took you off of your medication. How do you feel?"

"OK."

"Do you hear any voices?"

"No."

Susan shook her head in an exaggerated fashion.

"OK, let's draw something today."

***

"We saw the judge the other day," said Ellen, talking on the phone to Edwin and looking through the visitor's window. "Mr. Aaron said it was a different judge from the one who you saw. It was time for your thirty-day review. Doctor Brinkerhoff was there and appeared on the witness stand. He said that you have schizophrenia and should remain confined to maximum security in the hospital. The judge set the review date for one year or before that time if circumstances dictate."

Chapter 10: Tragedy Redux

Three months had passed. Things had become pretty much routine. Oh, there was still the art therapy. There were the fights. Not having weapons made the men less formidable and more controllable. There were the televisions and the radios. And there were the cigarettes. The guards had to remind each man as he went by, "Put out your cigarette. Put out your cigarette. What you got in your hand, man? Put out your cigarette. I gotta tell you a thousand times. Put out your cigarette."

But hardly anyone ever got to see the doctor.

"Is there a doctor?" everyone would ask.

At times it was rumored that someone had actually seen one, but Edwin had not seen anyone since his one encounter several months ago.

But now it was nighttime. Edwin was busy in his cell on ward two – drawing pencil sketches using the book his father had bought for him and getting better at it every day. Fellow patients had come to him, asking him to draw their portraits so that they could send them to their girlfriends outside. And so he did for free and apologized for making them look like Frankenstein's monster. They said that they didn't mind.

But he was still crazy, the right side of his brain going into all sorts of uncontrollable flights of fantasy, and the left side arguing logically and intensely against them. Edwin dropped onto his bed exhausted every night.

Tonight was no different, so it seemed. He pulled himself away from his drawing to argue with himself.

Then suddenly, "You lost your mind."

And just as suddenly all was quiet.

"You lost your mind," it repeated.

Edwin could not breathe as the Truth dawned upon him: He had lost his mind. They had told him. They had told him that he was not well. Neither of those who had suffered – his wife, his son – had suffered for any good reason. A dark and terrible illness had blinded his eyes and only now revealed to him the destruction that he had wrought. He was alone, locked in a cell in a world of despair.

Edwin wept bitterly.

***

At his next visit with his parents Edwin told them that he realized that he had lost his mind. They were relieved for this much, but they told him that he would have to go to trial. Ellen cried for her son.

Part 2 (of 8)

The Trial

Chapter 11: Keenan's Legislation

Assemblyman Glenn Keenan had introduced legislation to make the mentally ill pay for their time in State hospitals, and now it was up for debate. And the debate was heated. The mentally ill were seen by some, as Keenan himself did, to be no better than criminals.

"It sounds like a 'you hold him while I hit him' tax scheme to me," said a detractor. "The Court will put the patient in the hospital against his will, and you're asking the State now to charge him for every minute that he is in there, and he has no recourse. A patient normally has the option of signing himself out if he can no longer afford his bill. The doctor may not like it, but he will do it. There is no such thing here."

"The patient can appeal to the Court," said Keenan.

"The Court will not take the responsibility for setting the patient free without the guidance and consent of the doctor."

"How much money are we talking about?"

"The sky is the limit. Some have been in the hospital for decades, running into millions of dollars. All of this must be repaid."

"And when he dies?"

"His assets – if there are any – go to the State. And if he is that rare individual who is married as well, the joint assets of the surviving spouse go to satisfy the lien."

"And leave her without support in her dotage?"

"Let's go back. I am seeking the assets of the patient to pay his bill, but as they usually have none, it becomes the responsibility of the family – if he has one. This bill will take the assets that the family planned to use to support him."

"And make him live in the streets? A cycle of thievery and incarceration just like the common criminal? Is that your plan? Your great plan?"

Someone said, "These guys have no assets. We usually write it off. What's the problem if we just provide the services at no charge?"

"It's not their money! It's our money!" retorted Keenan.

With a shout the debate ended in a fight on the debating floor.

The bill passed by a moderate margin.

Chapter 12: Officer Castellano at Home

It was a fine summer's day. The humidity had tapered off. The sun was shining. A gentle breeze blew, and birds chirped in the trees. Ah, it was beautiful. Frank Castellano and his wife could not have chosen a better day to celebrate the birthday of their young son, now two years old, with a backyard barbeque with their relatives.

In the meantime, the children were playing a game of keep-away, and the young boy wanted to play as well. As expected, no one gave him the ball, and he wailed ever so pitifully. So one of the girls gave him the ball which stopped the tears while he held onto it. Everyone encouraged him to throw the ball, which he did, but no one gave it back to him. So again he wailed pitifully and searched for his father who picked him up and comforted the boy on his shoulder.

"He needs his Daddy," said his wife.

Chapter 13: Aaron and Edwin Confer

It was at this time now at Edwin's recovery of his senses that Daniel Aaron made the trip to State Hospital to speak with him and make their plans for the trial.

"The prosecutor Georgia Bailey will ask for capital punishment – the death penalty – when we stand before the judge. She is, however, willing to plea bargain with you. She is willing to let you serve thirty years in prison without parole. Our other option, and we have begun to build our case upon it, is an insanity plea, but there is no knowing how the jury will decide these things. The success rate of insanity pleas is about one-quarter of one percent. You're an engineer, so you can see that the odds are stacked against you greatly if you choose this option. The decision is yours. How do you plead?"

Edwin thought silently wishing that it would all be over. He said, "I will plead insanity."

"If you win the case you will always have the stigma of being mentally ill and treated as such by the Court. You will also be a second-class citizen in society."

"I don't want to plead guilty to something that I didn't want to do."

Aaron was taken aback and thought nervously for a minute.

"All right, then. We will plead insanity. I wish you luck."

Chapter 14: Doctor Brinkerhoff's Opinion

In early November Edwin was called to the dining room by Doctor Brinkerhoff.

"I spoke with your attorney today in preparation for the trial. What do you think is going to happen?" asked the doctor.

"I don't know. This is new to me, and I can't make guesses anyway."

The doctor smiled.

"I'm certain that you will do all right. I'm going to recommend your release."

"It's a little early, isn't it?"

The doctor ignored him.

"What therapies are you involved in now?"

"Art therapy and movement therapy."

"I want you to get some work therapy as well – a job in the dining room. It's not much, but it is the most that we can offer."

"Thank you."

"I'm sure you will do well."

The doctor left, and Edwin was escorted back to the Day Room.

The weekend came, and Edwin was called out for the weekly visit with his parents. This time his sister Sasha as well as Larry Cisco were with them.

"Do you remember Larry?" Sasha asked.

"Yes," said Edwin.

"He is my husband now. I wanted you to know before anything happened."

Edwin was silent.

Sasha continued, "We also had a wedding picture made for you – unframed – so that you can have it after you get out. Here, look."

She held up the available light shot that was taken in the church with her in her gown and Larry in a tuxedo.

"What do they have you doing in there?"

"Nothing. I go to a couple of therapies once per week. They're talking about having me work in the dining room. Otherwise a lot of time sitting around"

"What about the other people? Don't they do anything for them?"

"Very few."

"Don't they have visits from their families?"

"In most cases their families have abandoned them. This is their home. There are maybe four or five guys who get visits out of the seventy or so."

So they all continued with some small talk for an hour until the visit was over. Edwin received his weekly fruit and shared it only with those closest to him. The remainder of the patients had been dubbed "vultures" by an observant patient who had his own problems, thinking of himself as the angel Gabriel, waiting for the order to blow his trumpet. The vultures only took and gave nothing in return.

The next day, Monday, the therapist in charge of the dining room gave Edwin an interview and, having been satisfied with his responses, offered Edwin the opportunity to work in the dining room. Edwin's father had encouraged him to take it. His rationale was, first, that it would give him something to do. Second, he could make a little money as the patients were paid for this type of work. Third, it would show that he could handle this much "job stress." Not everyone could. His duties would be to help set up for meal time, serve the meal, and then help to clean up and to mop the floor.

One of the first things that happened as he was wiping the tables was that another patient, John Durocher, came over to him and threatened seriously to kill him.

"Kill me, then," was the standard response that everyone used with the hope that maybe someday somebody would and just put the victim out of his misery. Edwin used it too. "You have family you want to notify first?" he added.

"I'm going to kill you."

And he left, leaving Edwin to avoid looking over his shoulder.

At the hospital there was an issue with smoking, the only vice allowed. Patients were not to have cigarettes in their cells, but they kept trying to sneak them in and smoke them there.

This particular night a patient succeeded in getting a lit one past the guards, and you could hear him laughing and joking in whispers to his friends.

After everyone was inside and the cell doors were locked, he smoked his cigarette. Then, out of casual interest, he tried to see if his mattress would burn. It would. Black smoke billowed out of his cell filling the dormitory as the flames grew higher. He was laughing no more. He was screaming in agony right next to Edwin's cell as he died in the flames. The gate to the cell jammed as the guards tried to save him and the rest of the patients. Edwin lay down on the floor to escape the thick, black smoke. Finally, all of the gates were opened, and the remainder of the patients was taken to a safe area. Emergency medics arrived on the scene, and the patient was taken by helicopter to a trauma center where he was pronounced dead.

Chapter 15: Georgia Bailey and the Press

Georgia Bailey continued her affair with the press. Her opinion of them was low, but she used them to her advantage.

"They'll write whatever sells. Here, there is the thriller of a defenseless society threatened by an insane killer. Our only protection is to apprehend him and execute him. I must protect society. I will see to it."

Chapter 16.1: The Trial – Part 1

The trial date was set for the second week of November in the same year as the incident. Daniel Aaron thanked Judge Washington for his graciousness in granting Edwin his right to a speedy trial. The judge also allowed Edwin to be housed in the local County Psychiatric Hospital during the trial rather than have him transported daily the long distance to and from State Hospital. This not only cut down on the State's transportation expenses but also made it easier for Edwin's parents to visit him. He was to remain on a locked ward, which was a far cry from the iron gates of the maximum-security facility at State Hospital. To Edwin it was like gasping fresh air after being under water for so long.

But not all was peaches and cream. Edwin's mother told him that the stories in the paper were cruel.

"Why are they doing this to me?" he thought in perplexity "I've never been in trouble with the law. I was in Boy Scouts. They printed the stories! I was a model citizen. And why do my parents tell me this now?"

"We're trying to keep you away from these things and let you get well," his mother continued, "but this time we thought maybe you should know."

***

On the first day of the trial the security officers from Health and Human Services arrived bright and early at County Hospital to put him in his chains and take him over to the courthouse. There he was taken up the back way to an area off of the courtroom and placed in a holding cell where the chains were removed at the request of Daniel Aaron to Judge Washington.

"To show consideration toward Edwin Potter's mother who will be present during the proceedings."

Meanwhile two court officers were standing to the side holding a quiet conversation as Georgia Bailey entered the court room wearing a dark blue pants suit.

"Here she is now," said one. "Miss Bluebird of Happiness."

"Maybe her mother dressed her funny as a kid."

Bailey finished putting down her folders and headed for the door leading to the holding cells. She went inside and found Edwin waiting quietly. She went up to the bars and told him that she saw nothing wrong with him.

"You are a murderer, and you will pay for your crime. I will see to it."

Aaron asked Edwin later what she said.

"She wants to see me die," he said flatly.

Aaron, suddenly slack-jawed, turned away from Edwin slowly, wondering if he really heard Edwin correctly. He left the area dumbfounded and returned to the courtroom.

When all parties were present for the day's proceedings, Edwin was brought out to the defense table and told to be seated. The jury candidates were not yet in the room. There were some preliminaries to be addressed beforehand which included the charges to be brought against Edwin Potter and the penalty that Georgia Bailey sought.

"The State brings one count of homicide in the first degree and two counts of assault with a weapon. We seek capital punishment."

"Mr. Aaron," started Judge Washington, "how does Mr. Potter plead?"

"Not guilty by reason of insanity, Your Honor."

The judge paused.

"All right. Bring in the jurors."

Roughly twenty-five people were brought into the courtroom. Edwin was numb. All anyone knew of him now was that he was an enemy of society. On TV shows it was always the other guy. Now it was Edwin whose fate lie in the hands of twelve of these people. As they filed in he wanted to say to them, "Don't you know me?" But each one took his seat with gravity and turned toward the judge.

And the process of selecting a panel began with the process of elimination. Several were excused on the moral grounds of opposition to capital punishment. One had a family member who had been involved with a trial in the past. A few had heard about the case in the news. That done the selection of twelve jurors and two alternates began by lottery, and the first number out of the box belonged to Glenn Keenan.

After the panel was agreed to, Judge Washington oriented the jurors. Then the trial began.

"We are going to take things a little bit out of order so that the witness can return to his duties," said the judge. "Mr. Aaron, would you call your witness, please."

"Thank you, Your Honor. For the Defense, Patrolman Francis Castellano."

Officer Castellano took the stand and, through questioning by Aaron, related his involvement with the arrest of Edwin Potter on the night of the incident. Finally, Aaron also asked about Edwin's character.

"Did he give you a problem that night?"

"No."

"He went peacefully?"

"Yes, and his father accompanied him."

"Has he ever been a problem to the community – in your recollection?"

"No."

"Has he ever been arrested – in your recollection – on a different occasion?"

"No."

"No further questions, Your Honor."

"Prosecutor?"

"How long have you been on the force, Officer?"

"About five years."

"No further questions, Your Honor."

Daniel Aaron later explained to Edwin that the Prosecutor did not want to tarnish the officer's uniform without warrant. It would only weaken her case.

Officer Castellano was dismissed, and the order of the proceedings returned to normal. The County Coroner appeared for the Prosecution attesting that the victim was dead and how she had died. In Edwin's mind Amy had been reduced to an object in a court battle. She was no longer a person, a far cry in Edwin's heart from the intimacy he had shared with her in their bed. Also appearing for the Defense was Edwin's next-door neighbor who testified that Edwin was a good husband and a good neighbor. Ellen Potter also appeared on the stand to testify that Edwin appeared "just wild" to her on that night, far from the usual sight of the son she knew. And that was it for the day.

***

The next day the doctors testified. Both doctors Brinkerhoff and Edmonds took their time to explain to the jury the indications they believed showed that Edwin was insane at the time of the incident, especially his belief that his employer wanted him to save a project for them or they would harm or kill his family. The doctor for the prosecution had something different to say.

"And would you tell us, please, Doctor, your impressions from your interview," asked Bailey.

"He was completely sane at the time."

"And why do you say that?"

"He has no insight to his illness. He does not know what caused it."

"What else?"

"When he was suffering from the effects of his – contrived – illness, he never went to a doctor to check it out."

"I see. No further questions."

Daniel Aaron fired his cross-examination.

"I understand, Doctor, that mental illness is transmitted from generation to generation in some families. Is that true?"

"Yes."

"Would you tell us, Doctor, if it is necessary for a person with an illness – any illness – to understand its causes before he seeks medical assistance?"

"I'm not certain what you are asking."

"Isn't that why a person goes to a doctor? Because he does not know?"

"Yes," the Doctor said hesitantly.

"That will be all, Your Honor."

And that was all of the testimony for the day.

Doctor Edmonds had a word with Daniel Aaron as Edwin stood nearby.

"I can see that the Prosecutor's doctor knows where his money is coming from. The medical profession at this time does not know, either, what causes mental illness. I'm going to have a few words with him before he ruins the reputation of the profession."

***

The next day Edwin was called to the stand by Daniel Aaron.

"Edwin Potter, did you do it?"

Edwin was undone. Absolute silence reigned in the court room. If only he could be somewhere else. He didn't want to do it. He thought he was saving his family. The eyes of fourteen jurors were upon him, waiting for a simple answer. An answer that would convince them and set him free. The evidence was against him. What was he going to do? Say no?

"Yes," he said weakly.

Chapter 16.2: The Trial – Part 2

The trial continued.

"Is there anyone in your family who has or had mental illness?" Aaron asked Edwin.

"Yes."

"Who?"

"My grandfather."

"I want the Court to remember that the doctor for the Prosecution already testified that mental illness is transmitted from generation to generation. No further questions."

Georgia Bailey stepped up.

"Tell the jury, Mr. Potter, where you got the weapon that you used that night."

"I-I don't remember."

Bailey waited. So did the jury.

"Did you have the television on?"

"I don't remember."

Bailey fumed as her case died. But she did have a confession of guilt before the jury. And maybe Edwin Potter's sudden bout of amnesia would place a doubt about his illness into the minds of the jurors.

"No further questions, Your Honor. The State rests."

There were then the final arguments presented to the jury by the Defense and the Prosecution. When they were finished, Judge Washington instructed the jury on their deliberations, and the latter filed into the jury room to deliberate. Aaron bent over to tell Edwin to stand still when the jury delivered its verdict. Edwin was returned to the holding cell to stare quietly while Aaron and Baily spoke with the judge.

After a few hours of deliberation, the jury foreman, a woman, had an issue for the judge. Everyone was brought back into the courtroom.

"What is the issue?" asked the judge.

"One of the jurors is strongly prejudiced against the Defendant and wants to sway everyone to vote for conviction."

Judge Washington fumed.

"What is his number?"

"Four-seven-three, Your Honor."

"Four-seven-three, stand up!"

Glenn Keenan stood up. Judge Washington glared at him.

"You are dismissed from further involvement in this case! Alternate number one, you will take his place."

"Your Honor --!" started Keenan.

"You are dismissed!" roared the judge.

Keenan left the room followed by his wife. Neither of them spoke. There was a smoldering tension between the two of them as they walked to their cars, got in, and drove home.

Chapter 16.3: The Trial – Part 3

When they got inside the house, Keenan's wife spoke first.

"You always have an answer, don't you?"

"It's my job to have an answer."

"And you don't have a problem coercing fourteen people to send a mentally ill man to his death, either."

"He was guilty."

"He was sick! Didn't you hear the testimony? No, you only hear what you want to hear."

"He was guilty! An eye for an eye and a tooth for a tooth!"

"I don't want to hear any more of it! You are a fool with a heart of stone! I am going to file for divorce. You will hear from my attorney."

"Fine! I'll be waiting!"

"And you're a cheapskate as well!"

And she left.

She did not come home that night. She went to stay at her mother's.

A few days later he received a letter in the mail from an attorney representing his wife in the matter of a divorce. He sat down and hung his face in his hands.

"How did this happen?"

Chapter 16.4: The Trial – Part 4

That afternoon the jury delivered its verdict: Not Guilty by Reason of Insanity. The case, previously known as *State v. Edwin Potter*, was now referred to as *In the Matter of Edwin Potter*. He was remanded to State Psychiatric Hospital, and the date of review was set for three months later.

Georgia Bailey was infuriated by the jury's decision and vowed that she would not allow it to stand. Her supervisor chased her into the ladies' room and gasped, "Prosecutor! Do you think that because you are an attorney and a prosecutor for the State that you can enter a Court of Law and deal out your own brand of justice? You are out of order! In this country we have the Rule of Law! No one is above the Law! He is protected by his right to avoid double jeopardy!"

"He is a murderer, and I must protect society!"

"The society you want to protect just acquitted him! If it is society you want to protect, then you must now keep him in the hospital as an incurable menace to that society!"

Georgia Bailey only fumed all the more, but an idea had been planted in her mind.

Chapter 17: The Death of Officer Castellano

Sometime later after the trial was over Officer Castellano was in the locker room at the station. There were comments to him that Edwin Potter had been found insane by the jury and acquitted.

The sergeant came in, saying, "Castellano! The lieutenant wants to see you!"

As Castellano got up and disappeared from sight, a shot rang out, and he slumped to the floor dying.

***

On their next visit to State, Edwin's parents gave him the news.

"It was said to be a gun-cleaning accident."

Edwin began to wonder faintly if his delusions did not have some basis in fact.

Part 3 (of 8)

Release from State Psychiatric Hospital

Chapter 18: Meet Adam Stein

In December of the same year as Edwin's incident and trial, Billy Anderson, a guard, let a patient, Jimmy Black, go free by Order of the Court. Anderson then went inside to the dining room – his next duty – to help prepare for lunch as Edwin overheard. Anderson sat at a table and complained to his co-workers about the release.

"I can't believe what I just did. Tell me I'm going crazy. I just let Jimmy Black go free. He has nothing going for him. No family. No friends – except his druggie street friends. No job. No education. No money. No place to live – not even a good shirt and a pair of pants.

"So here is where I'm crazy. I gave him a five-dollar bill out of my own pocket and a cigarette, lit it, and told him not to kill anybody. And I'm even more generous. I give him three days – three days! – before he's back."

Jimmy Black was back in two days.

"You didn't kill nobody, did you?" Anderson asked him. "No? That's good. You're always welcome here. Let's go to the Day Room."

"Some guys have no home," continued Anderson in his running conversation those two days later in the dining room with his co-workers. "This is their home and family. Then there is that minister inside with the green suit. He got out of prison just filled with the Holy Spirit and was gonna give people God's Word, but nobody told him that he was gonna have to feed himself. 'Oh, consider the ravens! They neither sow nor reap, but God feeds them! And how much more are you worth than the birds?' They caught him trying to beat it out of a man on the street in the City."

Edwin was also in the dining room those two days later. There was one patient who came to work the other day, did one meal, and left. He couldn't handle the pressure. Today there was an enormous man called, aptly, Big Man who started to lose his composure as they set up for breakfast.

From behind the steam table Big Man called out to Billy Anderson, "What happened, Billy Anderson? What happened? Yesterday I was out there a free man! Walking to my job and taking care of my family. Now I'm in here! Accused of battery! What happened, Billy Anderson? What happened?"

And as he talked he rattled the pans louder with each passing moment. Anderson called him over.

"Here, my man. Take a seat. Let somebody else do that. You got a cigarette?"

Big Man took a pack out of his pocket and pulled one out. Anderson pulled out his lighter and lit the thing.

In only a moment the call went out and patients began to file in for breakfast, queuing up at the steam table (which for safety reasons was never turned on), receiving the food on their trays, and then heading for a seat at a table. One patient with a do-rag on his head stood up and angrily threw his tray to the floor, cursing non-stop. He was led away to a quiet room by a guard.

When the patients were done eating, a guard came around with a bucket and collected the spoons. They were counted, and, when the number matched the number given out, the patients were led to the Day room. Edwin still had a problem with John Durocher.

Once done in the dining room the patients were given the chance to visit the canteen where they could spend the money that they had earned for snack items and a few special items such as batteries for their radios. Frank Kirkland manned the store, well-versed in satisfying his customers. Edwin usually bought chocolate-covered peanuts and took the opportunity to use the pay phone to call home. When he was done with that he would usually go to the Day Room and sit and wait.

But this afternoon was different. As Edwin returned to the Day Room he found someone new at the table, someone with a shoulder bag. Who carried shoulder bags?

"I'm Adam Stein," he said to the group. "I just got off of Ward seven."

"It's good that you're off," said Frank, now off of work. "What are you here for?"

"I don't want to talk about it, but they say it was murder."

"Did you do it?"

"I don't remember. I was sitting home one night with my wife, and a police officer came to the door, showed the warrant, put handcuffs on me, and took me away."

"Are you Jewish?" asked Dom Sanchez.

Here Stein hesitated.

"Yes," he said.

"Have you told anyone?" asked Frank.

"No. This wouldn't be the first time in history where a Jew is locked up in a maximum-security facility for psychiatric observation. Why start trouble?"

"What did you do for a living?"

"I'm a TV repairman."

So the group pointed out different people in the room including Roger Breakstone.

"Does anybody play an instrument?"

"I played a little guitar," answered Edwin. "Why?"

"My wife plays violin, and I was just wondering."

"Adam Stein!" called a guard at the gate. Then catching his eye, "You got a visit."

"Probably my wife," said Adam. "She's quick. I'll try to make the best of my situation. I hope she has a newspaper."

Chapter 19: Church

"Church! Catholic deacon!" cried the guard at the gate to let the patients in the Day Room know that church services were now available.

"Church! Catholic deacon! No more than eight!"

Edwin got up and found himself included among the eight. Now familiar with the process, Edwin and the other seven were taken along the walkways and the stairs – always punctuated with iron bars and gates – until they arrived at a room with a man dressed in Catholic vestments. Here, too, after the patients and guards filed in, the gate was closed and locked.

One of the patients stood up and clamored, "The Pope is the anti-Christ --!"

"Stop there," said the deacon. "The Pope is not the anti-Christ. That is hate speech!"

"Jesus was a black man!"

"You're going to have to be quiet or you're going to have to leave," said a guard.

"I'll be quiet. I won't be no problem."

"All right, then. Today I want to read from one of the gospels, and then I want to distribute the Eucharist."

The Paulist deacon read the story of Lazarus from John's gospel, and made the connection according to Saint Jerome that his death and return to life through Jesus was to be used as a miracle in a manifestation of the glory of Christ for those who believe. It is a story of hope and God's love.

Having given the homily, the Eucharist was next. And the hosts were distributed to the faithful.

The deacon done, the patients were led back to population, and, for the moment, just a little bit different from when they left.

Chapter 20: Plans and Occupations

With the Mass now over and the patients back in the Day Room – still too cold for any fresh air, Jerry English, a patient, stopped by Edwin's table to tell his story starting with the anguish that his medication was causing him. Maybe there was truth in it. His face was always contorted, and he walked with his arms held out before him from the waist, bent at the elbow. English, like so many others, hated it at State hospital. He hated the medical treatment, and he hated the social aspects. He hated being treated as a second-class citizen. He wanted out.

"Just like everybody else whether they say it or not," he said.

English felt that he was different. He had a plan, but he would never tell anyone what it was. He swore, though, that he if he ever left the hospital he would return only at gunpoint. At this point he would turn and leave to wander in the Day Room.

Other patients were playing cards with Rex Walker or watching TV shows – dubbed by Adam Stein as "television therapy" as there didn't seem to be much else available in the way of therapy. Still others were standing around smoking or telling stories of their own about sex, drugs, alcohol, women, hanging out on street corners, Hitler, Nazis, Nazis in Argentina,

Jews, jail, prison, and anything else that was unacceptable in society. Never about a job that any one of them had had – except one. He had a bowl-cut haircut and a strange look in his eye. He complained about the Prosecutor.

"I had a job driving a truck. Minding my own business. And the Prosecutor went and told my boss that I have mental illness and was a danger to society. So the State took my CDL from me, and I had no place to go. Couldn't support myself. Couldn't support my wife and family. So I robbed a loaf of bread from a supermarket, and they put me in here. I don't know what I'm gonna do now."

Edwin thought about it but didn't know whether to believe him or not considering where he was.

At this point Edwin overheard Jamal from across the room. Jamal liked being in the hospital.

"Three meals a day, a warm and dry place to sleep."

"We're gonna have to send you out real soon," said a guard. "This is not a hotel."

"Well, I want to stay here because I know that God has a plan for my life."

"What's the plan?"

"I don't know, but God has a plan for my life!"

Rex Walker overheard Jamal and reared back to have his say.

"These motherfuckers don't amount to nothing! I can get more from shit -- !"

Slick was right in his face, knocking Walker backwards and onto the floor with a hard thud, knocking him out. Walker didn't move.

"Get up, motherfucker!" they could barely make out from Slick.

Whistles blew everywhere, and patients were rushed to their cells. Slick was brought to a quiet room before he was moved to Ward seven.

Chapter 21: Patient Advocate

Paul Gregory was still raging against "the Administration," Jacob Schmidt in particular. These two were now face-to-face. Gregory was in Schmidt's face about the patient who had died in the mattress fire, using it as an indictment against, as he said, "the inept and incompetent patient care practices of Jacob Schmidt and this hospital."

Schmidt countered calmly that an investigation had been done, and, despite the responsible actions of the guards to enforce the no-smoking policy in the private cells, this one patient was able to sneak a cigarette through. The only other course of action would be to ban cigarettes altogether.

"Do you smoke, Gregory?"

Yes, he did, and they knew it.

Gregory countered with the release to the streets of patients who were completely unprepared, citing the return of Jimmy Black who was back after being gone for only two days. Schmidt responded that it was beyond his control who gets released, that it was between the doctor and the Court.

Gregory was livid that Schmidt had the answers to all of his questions and swore that he was going to kill him. Schmidt responded that if anything happened to him, Gregory would be the first one who they would come after.

Gregory argued that the newspapers should be brought in so that the outside world could see what went on at State. Surprisingly, Schmidt agreed that it was a good idea and suggested the TV news program "One Hour of Your Time."

Gregory agreed heatedly.

Chapter 22: First Review Hearing

The time had come now for Edwin to return to the Court for his first review hearing. Before the proceeding Daniel Aaron confided to Edwin that Judge Washington did not like Georgia Bailey.

"In the Matter of Edwin Potter," called the Judge.

"Your Honor," said Bailey, "there was a fire at the records warehouse, and the State is limited in what it can present to the Court today. I would ask for a postponement."

The judge thought for a moment.

"Mr. Aaron, are you and your client ready?"

"Yes, Your Honor."

The judge thought some more.

"Ms. Bailey, you are well-versed in this case having followed it from the beginning as Prosecutor. We will proceed. I will give you ten minutes to prepare, and we will begin."

The judge left the bench, and the Prosecutor and Defense attorneys found themselves standing elbow-to-elbow at the Defense table, now facing Edwin.

Aaron asked quietly, "Did you start the fire, Georgia?"

Georgia Bailey was shocked to find herself under interrogation.

The hearing was brief. First, Georgia Bailey ripped into Edwin.

"Tell us, Mr. Potter, have we jogged your memory?"

With a moment's hesitation, Edwin replied, "Yes, you have. And you, Georgia Bailey, have made me remember things that I do not wish to remember!"

Suddenly everyone was nervous. Daniel Aaron walked slowly to the Defense table. Bailey's voice was a bit higher.

"No more questions, Your Honor."

Aaron called Doctor Brinkerhoff to the stand.

"Would you give us the status of the patient, if you would please, Doctor."

"Mr. Potter is in stable condition. He shows no signs of psychosis. He functions at the level of a professional which he is."

"What do you recommend for him?"

"I still believe that his release from the hospital is appropriate."

"Would you recommend visitations with his infant son given that the Court may not be fully ready to release him yet?"

"Oh, yes! I would recommend monthly visits under strict supervision at the hospital."

"Why do you say 'strict'?"

"It is a maximum-security facility, and that is the way that things are done. There is no prejudice against Mr. Potter."

"Thank you, Doctor."

Georgia Bailey began her questioning.

"Doctor, how long ago did the incident occur that brought us here today?"

"In July of last year."

"Which is roughly less than a year?"

"Yes."

"Isn't this a very short period of time given the severity of the actions performed by Mr. Potter?"

"No."

"Why not?"

"Recovery does not always require a long period of time. Some patients, for example, have been medicated and under treatment for decades with no real improvement in their condition. Some others recover quicker. Mr. Potter falls into this latter category."

The examinations concluded, Aaron made a brief argument to the judge.

"State case law," and he cited some, "requires that a patient be put in the least restrictive environment that he can handle."

Georgia Bailey posited that Edwin is now a menace to society and should never be set free, an about face from the position that she took during the trial.

Judge Washington, having considered the testimony and the arguments, ordered that Edwin continue his stay at State Hospital for another six months but allowed Edwin monthly supervised visits with his parents and son at the hospital, recognizing the studied improvement a child could make upon his parent.

Chapter 23: Patient Discipline

Back in the hospital Frank was in trouble. He was accused of stealing money from the canteen.

"Where is it?" asked the guards.

"That's what I would like to know!" Frank replied. "Nothing up my sleeve!"

"This is a serious matter, and it will go on your record."

"I didn't take it! I don't handle money! I debit their accounts by writing the transaction on a sheet of paper — Oh, you didn't think of that!"

After more of this, Frank said that it was in his mattress. The guards cut open the mattress and found nothing. They accosted Frank again.

"How would I cut open the mattress? We're not allowed to have anything that will hurt someone." Frank pleaded, "Why do you believe that and not that I didn't take the money?"

"All right, who took it?"

"Staff!"

Frank was put on Ward seven.

.

Chapter 24: Art Therapy II - Intern

Some days later Frank was released from Ward seven and returned to his previous cell, just in time for Art Therapy. That day there was a young woman in attendance. The patients had been told for a few weeks that there would be an intern joining them.

"I guess this is she," thought Edwin as he took a seat at one of the picnic tables in the dining room. Susan had not yet introduced her.

The young woman moseyed her way over to Edwin and started up a conversation.

"What's your name?" she asked.

"Edwin Potter."

"I'm slumming. I won't ask what you're here for. Most people have some pretty serious issues to deal with."

"Yeah," responded Edwin, raising his eyebrows.

"When do you think you'll be getting out?"

No one had asked him that before. Maybe there was an interest here worth developing.

"Well," he started, "I stood trial back in November and was found Not Guilty by Reason of Insanity. The doctor recommended my release to the judge, but the judge isn't buying it yet."

"Well, I do know what you're here for. Do you have a job?"

"I'm an engineer."

"But unemployed nevertheless."

"I've had a few issues to deal with recently. Can you wait?"

The intern took a seat next to him at the table which, unable to support both of them, fell sideways, dumping them to the floor and returning upright with a loud crash. Guards started to run over, but, seeing no threat, remained only wary. The romance was over.

Susan, having regained her composure, took this opportunity to introduce the young woman who was seated now by herself at a different table.

"I want to introduce you to Sandra. She is an art therapy intern and will be with us for a few weeks."

"Hi," said Sandra.

"Frank," began Susan, coming around the table, "what happened earlier this week?"

Frank sighed in exasperation.

"Putting me in a good light already for the intern... I stole some money – they say."

"Did you take it?"

"NO! I did not take it! – Well, maybe I did."

"What did you do with it?"

Frank shouted sarcastically, "I bought drugs with it – fifteen hundred milligrams of Thorazine!" And he laughed.

Adam piped up, "I don't think drug abuse is funny."

"Don't knock it if you haven't tried it."

"That's a stupid argument. If your mother tells you not to drink the bleach because it will kill you, are you going to try to prove her wrong?"

Susan gave Frank a look, waiting for his response.

"What about you, Stein? What are you here for?"

"I can't remember anything."

There was silence. Susan decided to change the subject. "Dom, what's new with you?"

"I decided to pursue my GED."

"That's a good thing."

"I just hope it's not too much for me. Some people don't want me to get it. They say it's a waste of time and money. I'm a little nervous – well, maybe a lot."

"Don't think about it," said Frank, "and you'll do all right."

"What about you, Edwin? You're usually pretty quiet."

"I listen. That's how I learn."

Susan shook her head in affirmation and thought about that.

Chapter 25: TV Interview

Later that day the TV news people showed up to do their interviews at State Hospital as demanded by Paul Gregory to Jacob Schmidt. Edwin was one of those chosen to be interviewed, but he was filmed only from behind: entering his cell and later during the questioning.

He was asked what it was like. Edwin responded that he had lost all of the respect he previously had as a contributing member of society. He was now seen as a peer of drug addicts and alcohol abusers with no future ahead for him. Any respect toward him made him feel like he was being accommodated, and he didn't like it.

After it was all over, they talked about it in the Day Room. Frank started.

"They come in, ask a lot of dumb questions, everybody says, 'Wow!', then they're done. They all go home, and nothing changes."

"What kind of dumb questions?" asked Adam.

"What does it feel like to be mentally ill? I had hoped for something better..."

"They don't know the answer to that question. They want you to help them out. Maybe it will help to restore all of us to sanity and get us home sooner."

Frank sighed in exasperation.

"They should ask, 'How do we fix it?' Would have been nice," he sighed.

"Do you know how to fix it?" asked Adam.

Frank gave a shrug, and things were quiet for the remainder of the afternoon.

Chapter 26: Doctor Desmond Edmonds, Part II

The next day, still cool in the early spring, Adam was reading his newspaper aloud in the Day Room about the crimes of "former mental patients" which was making it more difficult for those in State Hospital – and others as well, he was sure – to be released. And he also read that State legislatures were passing bills to spend more money to build more prisons. There was a building boom.

Gregory growled at him, "What about it? They'll put everybody in prison. Then what?"

"Then we'll all be in prison."

Paul Gregory had had enough of this logic and declared that Stein would be next on his list after Schmidt.

"What about Schmidt?"

"I'm gonna kill the bastard!"

"Why don't you just jump him the next time you see him?"

"Stein, I'm gonna…"

His words trailed off as he shook his finger.

Suddenly there was a commotion at the gate. Stan was being questioned by a guard who got on his radio and called the Control Center. Apparently there was a problem with a doctor:

Doctor Desmond Edmonds. Stan reported that the good doctor had a gun in his briefcase.

"How do you know this?" asked the guard.

"He told me, and I asked him to show it to me."

"Did he show it to you?"

"Yeah."

The doctor was apprehended and searched. A gun was found in his briefcase, and he was locked in a cell until police arrived. His days as a licensed psychiatrist were over.

Chapter 27: Fun and Games

Most of the time Edwin was like everyone else in his group: He waited and took catnaps. At one of his visits, Edwin's father commented about Edwin's social behavior.

"It's not good to be alone all of the time. You've got to go out there and meet people. Maybe someday – not right now – you'll find the right one. But this is not it. That was a terrible thing that you did."

Edwin felt nothing from society through the news media except the hatred and loathing. There was nothing he could have done almost a year ago. He didn't understand at the time. Now he had the burden to live with, to be reminded of it constantly. There would be no forgiveness – ever.

A few weeks later there was the monthly event called "Fun and Games" where girls from the local colleges volunteered to come in one night and spend an hour with the patients.

"Just don't tell my mother!"

Edwin tried it once, but while he was trying to make conversation other men barged in and tried to get a phone number and a date. It was embarrassing to him, making him feel like he was being identified with these graceless people, so he never went again.

Chapter 28: A Visit with Denny

"Edwin Potter!" called the guard.

Edwin got up from the table in the Day Room and walked over to the guard.

"You have a visit."

The gate was unlocked for him, and he passed through. He was escorted down the hall as he had been at least a thousand times before. This time they passed the glass windows and turned into the room that he remembered meeting Father Daley over half a year ago. Nothing had changed much, if any, but apparently someone had made an attempt to present a homey appearance.

As Edwin waited, the gate opened again, and Denny entered the room wearing a jacket and carrying his favorite plush toy with Derek and Ellen close behind.

"Look, Denny! There's your Daddy!"

Denny walked over as children do and gave Edwin a hug around the knees. Edwin hugged him back as tears formed in his eyes, being careful not to be too demonstrative. There was so much that this little guy had been through. His point was not to alarm the guards.

Edwin took the toy and started to play with Denny. Denny, seated on the floor, laughed and giggled. Then all of a sudden he lost his balance and fell backward, hitting his head on the floor. Denny wailed and went to his grandmother while Edwin looked on in terror, fearing that this would be his last visit with Denny.

The guards looked up.

Derek spoke up, "Denny fell backwards and hit his head. He lost his balance. He's just a kid. He just fell backwards."

The guards, having observed all of this, agreed. They allowed the visit to continue.

"Does anyone else ever get a visit?" Derek asked Edwin as they tried to settle down.

"Only Adam and Frank and one other guy, as far as I know. Everybody else is abandoned by family and friends. There's a reason for that comment in Matthew 25."

"Denny's godmother comes to see him every week or so. You remember Amy's friend?"

"Yes."

"Here. We brought a coloring book and some crayons."

"OK, Denny! Let's color!"

Chapter 29: Jazz

After the visit with Denny, Willie Green asked Edwin to attend his jazz history class. Edwin said yes and was led to the dining room where the class began with just a few others.

"Jazz has its roots in the black experience. And this right here, this place is part of it. Jazz started right here in America with the slaves. Some people don't want to hear that.

"The simplest thing to tell you about is Call and Response. It's how the message got out to those in the field. You can hear the style on some of the old popular tunes on the radio – like Motown! The first group would hear the message, and then they repeated it down the line to the next group, and so on..."

Willie Green also made the comment that he was doing this on his own time.

"There are some who don't want to see patients get educated. It's a fight every step of the way."

"Do you have a band?" someone asked.

"Yeah! Yeah! Five-piece."

"Can we hear them?"

"Administration won't let them in. I'm not supposed to tell you about security. But what we can do is get the patients to put on a show! Who plays an instrument?"

Edwin, along with a few others, raised his hand. He was not one who would be completely comfortable on a stage, but this would be his chance to shine, to feel normal again, to feel the instrument in his hands again if only for the matter of half an hour or so. To hell with Durocher.

"Good! I'll make the arrangements!"

The next week Willie came back with the good news that the show would go on. It would be in the dining hall. Each patient would play one tune.

"How about an encore?"

"Listen, we're lucky enough to get this much."

So somewhere they found various instruments for the patients and a folk guitar for Edwin for the day of the show. And right up in the front of the audience was John Durocher, looking like he was fit to kill and rush the stage. It didn't matter; Edwin's guitar made a good weapon now.

Edwin's turn came, and he sang a jazzed-up version of "Sunny" that someone had taught him years before. And when he was done, the crowd went wild, and – to Edwin's astonishment – John Durocher led the cheers. The man never bothered him again.

Chapter 30: Engineering

Adam Stein, with his bag eternally over his shoulder, sat down excitedly at the table.

"My wife bought me a programmable calculator! Would you like to see it?"

"Sure," said Frank.

Adam pulled it out of the bag as Edwin and the others watched.

"I'm wondering what to do with it. I'm thinking of designing a tone control for the stereo."

"How are you going to build it?" asked Frank.

"My wife is pretty good with a soldering iron. But I need somebody who can help me with the design." He turned toward Edwin. "You're an engineer. Would you help?"

"Does it do complex numbers?"

"What's that?"

"Let me see the thing."

So Adam gave it to Edwin who looked it over.

"I can derive the transfer function for the circuit that you give me and switch between rectangular and polar coordinates."

"I don't know what that means, but can you do it?"

"Yes."

"Great! Let me get some circuit ideas."

Chapter 31: Female Patients

Spring came. Adam Stein, who also worked now in the kitchen, was throwing out loaves of bread. Billy Anderson, thinking that Stein was breaking down, asked him for the reason.

"Those are the ones with the mouse droppings."

"Show me."

Adam showed him.

"Oh. Okay."

Then Anderson went and whispered to his co-worker that they had never checked that before.

"He makes a mean cup of coffee, too."

"I heard that Rex Walker will be back in about eight weeks. They say he's a changed man."

Some of the windows of the dining room faced onto the women's outdoor area, and one of the female patients was nearby. While Edwin mopped the floor, the other men called out to the woman and asked her to show them what she had – and she did to the cheers of the men. A female guard came over to pull the woman's clothing together and instructed her on sex and giving herself to the right man – not these men, Edwin included.

Chapter 32: Art Therapy III

"So, Dom," asked Susan, "what's new with you?"

"I have my GED now. I feel good."

"I heard," she said. "Congratulations."

"Now all he has to do is lose weight," said Frank.

"And I don't have to pay attention to turds like Frank Kirkland anymore to bolster my self-esteem. I'm my own man now."

Frank stared angrily. Susan watched the drama climax. Adam changed the subject.

"I designed a tone control for my home stereo. My wife put it together and said that it works great! And Edwin helped me," he said, pointing at Edwin.

Susan went into shock. Her jaw hit the ground. Patients weren't supposed to be capable of anything. She strolled over to Edwin.

"So you're pretty smart there."

"I went to school for it."

"It's a shame your trial is over."

"Mental illness and mental retardation are two different things. You should know that. Now I'm going to tell

YOU something: I am not a second-class citizen. I am just as good as any of you in here."

Susan began to respond.

"Oh, of course you are," Edwin filled in for her.

Then he read her the Riot Act, asking the questions and filling in all of the pat answers. Then all of a sudden Susan stood up. All of the pieces had fallen into place.

"Phone call," said the guard quietly as Susan left the room.

After about five minutes Susan returned a changed woman.

"Let's talk about something else," she said. "Does anyone know what is going on with Paul Gregory?"

"He thinks he's going to get away with something, but he tells everybody about it. And how is he going to do it? He's locked up in here with the rest of us. I wish he would just shut up," said Adam.

"I prefer that he keeps on talking," responded Susan.

Chapter 33: Summertime

Summertime arrived again. Edwin had been at State Hospital now for about two years. And he had noticed the conflicts over how the patients should be treated. Some felt that "hanging was too good for them. Show no mercy." Others felt that they were people with problems.

So amid this confusion a decision was made to have a barbeque for the patients for the Fourth of July holiday. A grill was brought into the yard and a lone woman cooked hamburgers and hot dogs. It was welcomed, but it was so bizarre in the setting of a maximum-security psychiatric facility not normally known for normal behavior.

When time had run out, the patients were escorted back to their wards. Edwin and Frank had been assigned to the same ward a little while back.

"I want sex with you," Frank murmured to Edwin.

"I'm not interested."

"Why not?" Frank demanded.

"Does it ever occur to you, Kirkland, that people have their own minds about things and what they want?"

"You should be open to trying new things!" he responded as they all entered their cells and the gates closed.

Edwin hoped that he would not have to kill this bastard.

Chapter 34: Paul Gregory

Paul Gregory still had it in his mind that Jacob Schmidt had to be eliminated. He rolled ideas over and over in his mind day and night. His staunch observations out his cell window finally yielded him the make, model, and color of Schmidt's car as well as its license plate number. He was so excited.

"I got it! I got it!" he reveled with those at the table in the Day Room.

"What do you have?" asked Adam.

"I have his license plate number!"

"You think you're going to get away with this. Everybody knows it's you."

"Circumstantial evidence!" he dismissed with a wave of his hand.

"Why don't you just hire a disgruntled military veteran as a hit man?"

Gregory gasped, "THAT'S IT!"

Chapter 35: Review Hearing and Release

Edwin went back to court for his regular annual review, and Judge Washington released him to County Psychiatric Hospital. He had spent two and a half years at State.

Part 4 (of 8)

Release from County Psychiatric Hospital

Chapter 36: The Death of Jacob Schmidt

Gene Allen, a former State patient now at County Psychiatric Hospital, got a telephone call from a friend at State Hospital.

"Jacob Schmidt is dead!"

The word spread like wildfire among the County staff.

"Jacob Schmidt is dead!"

"What? No!"

"He was murdered!"

"What? Murdered?! Oh, Lordy! Oh, Lordy! Who did it?"

***

Paul Gregory was seated before the panel at State Hospital.

"We know that you had everything to do with the death of Jacob Schmidt, Gregory."

"You got nothing on me. I'm trapped in this building like everybody else. How did I get out to do it?"

"We know you have Schmidt's license plate number."

"Circumstantial evidence!"

"You also threatened to kill him."

"So what? Circumstantial evidence! People threaten each other all over the place!"

"We also monitored your phone calls."

The speaker let the words settle in.

"We find you permanently insane, beyond our abilities to treat you with today's medicine. You will be sedated, like Roger Breakstone, and denied any contact with the outside world."

"You can't do that! I'll call my lawyer!"

"Call him. We did, and that's what we agreed to. The judge will see it that way too." Then a word to the guard, "Take him away."

Chapter 37: Meet Ruth Nussbaum, RN

Edwin spent sixty days on the Admissions ward at County Hospital. At the next hearing Judge Washington ordered that Edwin be moved from Admissions to a less restrictive but still locked ward and still have supervised visits with Denny once per month. Edwin had endured the cacophony, the cigarette smoke and smell, and a few psychological evaluations in a warehouse environment. He had also gotten the word of Schmidt's death.

The newspapers were now printing stories about how "former mental patients" were terrorizing communities by attacking innocent people, making it more difficult for Edwin or any of the patients to gain any freedom. What made it worse was the staff's stereotyping of him as an above-average but dangerous mental patient. Overcoming all of this would take time. He lived his life with regret, but he had been given his life by the jury. Now he must forge ahead if throwing his life away in these human wastelands was actually getting ahead.

After six months on the locked ward the judge moved Edwin to this open-door coed ward.

Ruth Nussbaum, a registered nurse and Head Nurse, was 46 and stood five-and-a-half feet tall with curly blonde hair and a pleasingly plump appearance – zaftig – by her own account. She was eating a jelly doughnut that one of the staff had brought in and had dropped some of it onto her blouse. Someone pointed it out to her. She looked down and tried to brush it away.

"I have jelly doughnut on my boobs!" she cried and wet a paper towel to try to wipe it off. She looked again. "Anything more than a handful is superfluous!"

She was also in the throes of a divorce and, in addition to swearing about her estranged husband, she acted like a drill sergeant.

One patient, Scotty, was delusional in that he believed his pinky was the cause of all of his problems and that if he cut it off he would be freed of his problems. This he mused aloud, obsessing over and over as he wandered through the ward. As he wandered past Ruth who was in the nurses's station, she put her cigarette down, pulled him over, and tried to console him.

"What's the matter bubelah? Why do you think like that?"

Gene came by as well and took him under his wing, telling Scotty that his thinking wasn't right, that he couldn't go on thinking that way.

"But you were free!" said Scotty in his child-like manner. "They let you go to work!"

"I couldn't handle the pressures of a job, but let's not talk about my problems."

"Okay... So you're back in the hospital."

"Yes, I'm back in the hospital."

For the moment Gene had succeeded in getting Scotty's mind off of his pinky, but in a few hours Scotty was back at it again.

Edwin happened to be standing near the nurses's station and heard all of this.

"You must be Edwin Potter," said Ruth.

"Yes," responded Edwin.

"Your reputation precedes you."

Edwin remained without comment. Ruth continued.

"I want to get to know you. Your chart from Admissions says that you have a flat affect and pent-up anger."

"What's a 'flat affect'?"

"It means that you don't express any emotion."

"What am I supposed to do? Smack somebody?"

"Ugh! Oy vey! They want to put you in Anger Management. What happened that night?"

Edwin related his story.

"That doesn't sound like anger. I'll talk with the Team, but first you have to learn to forgive yourself. Your wife is all right. Let me tell you a story. My ex-husband and I – schmuck!" she whispered, "were in the car racing down the road and having an argument. He took his eyes off the road, and we ran off the road, hit a tree, and the engine came in on us. Suddenly there was a tunnel of light, and there was peace. I started to go toward it. But then I remembered that it was my daughter's birthday, and I said that I couldn't go. Then I was back in the car with the ambulances around us. I had lost my nose, and the doctors had to sew it back on."

She looked cross-eyed at her nose.

"It was an NDE, a near-death experience. And all I want to say to you is that if there is that much caring about people in the afterlife, I'm sure that she is well taken care of."

A woman entered the ward and went over to Ruth.

"Do you have any folders here? We're all out of them on the ward, and I don't want to make the long walk to the Main building."

"See Hope. Oh, Sherry! I want you to meet Edwin Potter." Making the introduction, "Edwin, this is Sherry O'Connor. She's an LPN – a nurse – on the ward in the next building."

"Hello," he said self-consciously.

"I wish you all the best. Let me get what I came for."

And she left to find Hope.

"Sherry is a friend of mine. We live together – and split the rent! You can't get much on a nurse's salary."

Tom and Mandy were leaving the ward together.

"Where are you two going now?" called Ruth.

"It's none of your business," replied Mandy.

Hope Gavin, the staff person who Sherry sought, said, "While you are in the hospital it is our business."

"We're adults, and the decisions we make are our own."

"You're in the hospital because you can't make those decisions responsibly! Where are you going?"

"To the canteen."

"Well, all right. But go there and come straight back. I want you back by two o'clock."

The two left without another word.

Also on this ward was a very heavy black woman, Marylou, who had a drinking problem. And when she drank, she got mean and violent. She had her eye on Edwin as a love interest.

Then there was Zoe who had strong opinions and a beautiful daughter who was not in the hospital. Zoe spent most of her time knitting. She had a male friend, also a patient, by the name of Ronald. Like Marylou, Ronald also had a drinking problem, but he got to be dangerous when he was euphoric.

Just recently one of the female patients had given birth to a child who had been taken away from her by the State and put into a foster home. Zoe voiced her opinion to Hope.

"The child should not have been taken away from her!"

"Zoe! She would not have been able to take care of it."

"What do you mean? All of us could have helped!"

"The hospital is not the right environment to raise a child!"

"She was happy! Maybe this was something that could have cured her! The hospital does not want to see its patients happy!"

"Zoe! Life is not always a series of highs. There are problems that she still has to face and is not capable of raising a child!"

"Who are you to say that?"

Zoe began to escalate the argument, and Hope requested a sedative from the doctor, and it was injected.

"Why did you have to do that?" asked Scotty.

"You have to know Zoe. She gets angry and out of control, so the injection is to help her."

To change the subject, Gene told Hope that he saw a big, heavy staff member kicking the geriatric patients on the deck of the building across the way. Along with several other patients Edwin supported him. That staff person was never seen again on the hospital grounds.

"Wait a minute, Edwin. There is a package for you. Miss Gavin!" called Ruth.

"Yes?"

"Where is the package from State for Edwin?"

"I know where it is. I'll get it."

Hope went to the back and opened up a closet. She reached in, pulled out a cardboard box and returned, giving it to Edwin."

"It's from a patient named Adam Stein. Do you know who he is?"

"Yes," responded Edwin, opening the box now that he had read the label. And inside the box was a clay sculpture of Adam Stein's face with a few tear drops.

"Looks like he misses you," said Hope. "You should write him a thank you note, and let him know you got it."

"Do you have anything that I can write with?"

Before he could get an answer the psychologist, Doctor Ginny Taylor, entered the ward and stopped at the nurses's station.

"I was looking through Edwin Potter's chart, and I saw that he is not on medication. Why is that? Everybody is on medication."

She saw him standing there.

"Are you Edwin Potter?"

"Yes."

"Why aren't you on medication?"

"The doctors say there is no indication for it."

"You're in the hospital. You should be on medication."

Edwin said nothing, worried that he would become a zombie like Jerry English or incapable of ever leaving the hospital.

Turning her attention back to Ruth, "Also there is no IQ test result in there."

"I took an IQ test at State," offered Edwin.

"There's no record in your chart. When are you available to take the test?"

"I'm ready now."

Doctor Taylor chuckled smugly, "That's a little soon for me. I'll get back to you sometime later this week." She turned to Ruth, "I'll have one of the psychology interns do it."

Done now she turned and went to the office to go about her business. The test was done a few days later, and the good doctor criticized the intern for being sloppy with the test. "Nobody who is mentally ill gets a score like that," she said.

Mental illness and mental retardation are not the same thing.

Chapter 38: Team Meeting

A few days later Ruth came to Edwin and told him that there would be a team meeting with the psychiatrist, Doctor Julius Luciano.

"He wants to recommend supervised home visits but no overnights because Denny lives there. He doesn't believe that the judge will go along with that. He also wants you to apologize to Amy's family. Your parents will be invited to attend."

So on the day of the meeting, a Wednesday, Edwin saw his parents arrive, and they talked about what was expected of them at the meeting. Derek and Ellen were called in before Edwin. Doctor Luciano wanted to get them to agree to home visits before he wrote his report to the Court. Derek and Ellen agreed.

The doctor also wanted to talk with them about the reason for their son's breakdown. At the time the belief was that insanity was the result of parental upbringing. Doctor Luciano swore by it.

"The apple doesn't fall far from the tree," he told Derek.

Derek, enraged, closed his mouth, and with Ellen in tow left the meeting.

Having no other option, the doctor called in Edwin.

"I want you to apologize to Amy's family."

"Will it bring Amy back from the dead?" Edwin asked sternly.

Doctor Luciano steeled himself.

"You don't understand. You show no remorse."

"What am I supposed to do? Emote for you on your command? And what about the one who follows you? And the ones after that? There has been no communication with the family. Let sleeping dogs lie."

"You are arrogant, Mr. Potter!"

"Ugh! Doctor Luciano, maybe I should talk with him in private," Ruth suggested hastily, kicking the doctor under the table.

Edwin was excused.

After Edwin left, Ruth continued, saying to the doctor, "This man has been through so much, yet he shows no signs of violence. He has no history of drug abuse or alcohol abuse, and neither violence nor abuse show up here at the hospital despite twenty-four-hour observation."

"I want to hear an apology."

"He seems to be pretty certain of what he will or will not do."

"I want to hear an apology."

"I'll talk with him."

"You can be his one-to-one as a... gift... from me to you."

"Ay ay ay!" she exclaimed and put her hands to her head.

She found Edwin in his room reading a book and asked if she could speak with him.

"Sure."

"Doctor Luciano still wants to hear an apology from you."

"How will it change anything? I didn't want to do it. You want me to go over there now and stir things up after years have passed? Re-open old wounds? Do you think it is guaranteed that they will forgive me and peace will reign?"

"Ugh! You know, it's not what you say; it's how you say it. Couldn't you just make nice with the doctor? Listen," she whispered. "He is afraid of you because you are so damned smart."

Edwin had never heard this before. He just listened.

"So he won't give in. I will speak with him and see what he will agree to."

So Ruth returned to the meeting, and Edwin waited, reading as he often did.

With time the door to the conference room opened as the meeting broke up. Ruth made her comments and then went to Edwin's room where she caught his eye.

"The doctor is willing to recommend supervised home visits. Your parents will supervise, and you can see your son again in a more normal setting. Isn't that good?"

Edwin was silent. He had never experienced graciousness while being deeply involved in an argument.

"But he says he will not recommend your release."

That was more like what Edwin expected.

Chapter 39: Home Visits Granted

It was late autumn, and Edwin appeared in Court for his annual review hearing. Daniel Aaron was there. His parents were there. So were Judge Washington and Georgia Bailey who always contended that Edwin continued to be a menace to society. She cited cases of the worst offenders in society to back her up. Edwin himself did not behave that way.

Edwin had been transported by officers of the Department of Health and Human Services and his hands had been tied by a leather belt. No chains anymore. The only difference was that Doctor Luciano was testifying on Edwin's behalf.

So the good doctor took the stand and defended his report and his recommendations. Edwin was progressing in his treatment, and the doctor – true to his word – recommended that Edwin be allowed three-hour home visits – mostly because of the travel time – but no overnights because Denny still lived in the house.

Judge Washington agreed to the recommendations, and Daniel Aaron agreed to write the form of Order for Judge Washington to sign which he did.

Chapter 40: A Taste of Freedom

After a few weeks the signed Order arrived at the hospital, and Derek Potter was told that he could make arrangements to take Edwin out for visits. So on his first Saturday out Edwin was told by his father that there was something wrong with him. Edwin disagreed. His father insisted all the more. Edwin withdrew from the argument. Then his father, in control, told Edwin that he had been enrolled in a life drawing art class at the community college, and they were on their way now. Derek walked Edwin to the door and told him that he would be waiting in the car. Edwin took his art pad that his father had given to him and walked into the classroom and took his seat. The instructor introduced himself and asked the model to do some 20-minute poses. She dropped her robe, and the class began.

An hour later the class ended, and Edwin met his father outside. From there they went home, and Edwin's mother smacked him in the back of the head. He pulled himself up to his full height and told her sternly not to hit him. She had the look of a wild animal in her eyes.

In the time that was left, he enjoyed – as he could – the remainder of his visit with his now five-year-old son. Denny was at the age where he could attend kindergarten. The best thing was that he seemed to show no signs of falling behind due to the attack three years earlier. Edwin was relieved. And to take it a step further, Edwin crouched down and told Denny quietly that the child was not the reason for his mother's death. At that Denny threw himself around his father's neck and held on tightly. When it was time to go Denny, in love with his father, lay down and grabbed Edwin's ankle, and Edwin had to drag him across the room. What could he say to a five-year-old to make him understand that his father could not – was not allowed to – stay any longer? All Edwin could do was to give a hug and promise to return.

Ellen, composed now, called to Edwin, "Your sister Sasha just gave birth to a baby boy, her second. His name is Peter. The first was born almost a year ago. His name is Richard. She and Larry didn't want to see you in the hospital because none of us knew what the patients would do when they saw her in her condition. And we didn't know how you would feel after all of the things you've been through. We thought it might be best just to let things lie, and you could see them when you got out."

The visits continued for about six months with Edwin taking art courses at a few different schools. He took color theory and composition, and life drawing. But soon the jig was up. Doctor Luciano happened to ask one day how the visits were going and what type of activities was being pursued. Derek told him the truth, and the doctor became livid.

"That is not what you are supposed to be doing! Edwin must be in your sight for your entire time together. He is not to go to school!"

"I didn't know," replied Derek. "No one told us how these visits were supposed to be."

"Well, that's the way they're supposed to be. All of us could go to jail if the judge hears about it! Now no more!"

"Whatever you say. Let me ask you this: Could he have a small drafting table in his room so that he can do some work for me?"

"What kind of work?"

"I have a commercial art business, and he would be working as an artist for me. You would be able to see for yourself what he is working on."

With a moment's thought the doctor agreed and walked away.

"No more!" he said.

Ruth caught the doctor on his way back to his office.

"Doctor Luciano, I want to take Edwin out to his wife's gravesite so that he can grieve and get it out of his system."

"No. He will not be able to handle it."

"What if I just take him to buy some clothes? He has been living in the same clothes since his arrest. He washes them on the ward, of course."

"Well, clothes-shopping is fine, but you are not to take him to the gravesite."

"As you wish," she said with a gracious bow.

The doctor restrained himself.

"When are you going?" he asked.

"As soon as you sign the pass."

"Bring it to me, and I will sign it."

So Ruth went and filled out a pass, bringing it to the doctor for his signature. True to his word he signed it. Ruth went to the ward to find Edwin.

"You and I are going out today to see about some clothes for you. OK?"

"I don't have any money for clothes."

"We can just look and see what is in style. It's been a while since you were out."

"OK. At least it will be off the ward."

Ruth and Edwin got into her car and drove off to town. Her first comment to him was that she was going to stop off at the cemetery to see where Amy was buried. She had done her homework beforehand and knew where the location was. Edwin was quiet while Ruth chit-chatted along the way.

They drove to the site and parked. Ruth was more serious now while Edwin got out of the car.

"It's over here," Ruth said while indicating an unmarked grave.

Edwin stood looking. Then the tears began, then great wails of grief as he fell to his knees and covered his face.

"She's dead! She's dead!" he cried through his tears.

Ruth was nervous. The doctor had been right. She tried to pull Edwin up from the ground.

"Let's go, Edwin! The doctor was right! He said that you would not be able to handle this! Please! Get up and come to the car!"

Weeping and sobbing Edwin pulled himself up slowly while Ruth still tugged at him and got into the car.

"Let's go back," she said. "I'll tell the doctor that you didn't have any money to buy any clothes. I'm sorry that I put you through this."

And they drove away in silence.

Chapter 41: The Story behind Edwin's Release

A week went by since that episode, and it was time for another team meeting, this time regarding Marylou. Marylou was pleasant when she was sober. She was from the Carolinas and had never completed high school. Doctor Luciano called her in to the meeting.

"How are you feeling, Marylou?"

"I'm feeling fine, Doctor. Since I don't drink no more I'm a changed person."

"I'm glad you said that because I'm considering making a recommendation to the judge to discharge you from the hospital."

"Oh, yes, Doctor Luciano! I have seen the error of my ways, and I won't drink no more! I swear by the love of Jesus!"

"Excellent!" cried the doctor. "I will make my recommendation for your release to the judge. You may go."

Marylou left. Ruth spoke up.

"She is playing you for a fool! Don't you see that?"

"Ruth, she's not that smart."

"She has street smarts! She knows how to survive."

"Oh, Ruth. I'm going to make the recommendation. I'm confident of the conversion of Marylou."

"Doctor, her problem is that she drinks, and when she drinks she gets violent. The reason why she hasn't attacked anyone here at the hospital is that there is no alcohol here for her to drink. What do you think she is going to do when she gets out of the hospital and alcohol is available to her?"

"No, Ruth. I've made up my mind that she is trustworthy."

"What about Edwin, then?"

"What about him?"

"I believe that he will not promise what he will not carry out. Will you recommend his release as well?"

"No. I told you that I expect something from him, and he will not give it. He will be here forever until he does."

With this the meeting broke up. Ruth could not contain herself as she left the conference room.

"'Oh, Doctor Luciano! I've seen the error of my ways!' The meshuggener doctor believes her! She's playing him for a fool!"

Hope changed the conversation.

"I was making notes in the charts and had the radio on. A patient formerly at State Hospital escaped from Pachaw State Hospital. His name is Jerry English. They said he had to be taken at gunpoint."

So the doctor went to Court and made his recommendation for the release of Marylou. Two days later she was back in Admissions at County. She had gotten drunk and attacked somebody.

"Will you make the recommendation for Edwin's release now?" asked Ruth.

Humiliated, the doctor said yes.

Ruth went to Edwin.

"The doctor is going to recommend your release at your next hearing, but they're not going to make it easy for you. You can't live with your parents because your son lives there, and you can't get Section Eight housing because of your Court status. And I don't recommend that you move back into your house in your old neighborhood. You'll be a target in the community. You will have to get your own apartment."

"How am I going to pay for an apartment without money or a job?"

"It will have to be done in steps. You will first need a job."

"I'm in the hospital. How am I going to find a job?"

"We will help you. Newspapers have want ads. I will buy you a newspaper, but you will have to get your own transportation – a car – so you can go on interviews."

"My father sold my car."

"Ugh! God will provide you with a car."

And so the discussion went. In early spring of that year the plan was presented to Judge Washington who approved it. Edwin was not allowed to have his own apartment yet, though. He had to remain in the hospital, and there was a curfew he had to submit to. Weekend visits to his parents and Denny were still allowed, but he still had to be picked up. Derek Potter was buying a new car, so Edwin was allowed to use the old one. As for dress clothes befitting a young engineer going on interviews, they were provided by his parents who had saved a few of his suits and brought them in for him to wear.

Edwin was not the only one with fashion problems.

"I don't have a thing to wear!" cried one of the female patients.

"What do you mean, Molly?" asked Mandy.

"Doctor Luciano said that I can look for a job, but I don't have a blouse that looks good enough."

"What size do you wear?"

Molly told her.

"Wait here."

Mandy disappeared into another room and in a few moments came out dressed in only a robe, holding out the blouse that she had been wearing only a moment before.

"I can't take this. What will you wear?"

"Don't worry about it. I can get another one."

She had given her the shirt off of her back.

Ruth had some advice now for Edwin before he began his job search.

"There is one thing to keep in mind when you're out there dealing with people. People will reject you outright if you say that you killed your wife. Tell them that she died in a car accident, and you weren't there. Let them get to know you first."

Edwin had to think about that. He wasn't one to lie. Wouldn't it be better to say that he had mental illness?

"And about your employment gap," Ruth continued, "tell them that you were working for your father's business. You were, weren't you? You have the drafting table in your room."

"Yes."

So Edwin was prepped for his first foray as one mentally ill into the world of work. Ruth bought some newspapers as she had promised, and both of them looked through the want ads until they found an opening in a nearby town. There was a telephone number, so Ruth let Edwin use the ward phone to ask for the interview which was granted. The next day he was on his way to the design and manufacturing facility of NLO, a local small business. They made radio components for both military and commercial applications – and he got the job.

Ruth then came to him with the information that representatives from both the Probation Department – Louise Tolston – and the Clinic for Mental Health – Doctor Howard Simon, a psychologist -- would come to the hospital at night once per week to start follow-up care for when he was discharged from the hospital. As it was explained to Edwin, it was only a technical matter that he was to see a Probation officer. That was just how the monitoring by the Court was to take place. Technically he was not on Probation.

Work went well. He did his job capably, and he was making friends at the lunch table. He was soon asked to take part in a research project, and he decided to use the on-line (pre-Internet) database that the Company invested in "so as not to re-invent the wheel." Also there was a Company picnic that he attended one Saturday. As he was still in the hospital, he needed to be escorted, so Sherry volunteered to hold the pass and attend the event with him.

Edwin was also seeing his follow-up care, and he could still see Denny with supervision.

Soon it was time to go back to Judge Washington to ask for discharge, and it was granted over the fright stories from Georgia Bailey – with one stipulation.

"Have you told your employer about your Court involvement?" asked the judge.

"No, Your Honor," said Edwin nervously.

"Your Honor, it would make him a target in the community," interjected Daniel Aaron.

"I want it done," said Judge Washington.

But despite this, Edwin was allowed to find his own apartment with the requirement that he must report to both Probation and the Clinic once per week. Fortunately for him they were willing to accommodate him at night after work.

So Edwin turned again to the newspaper and looked at its real estate listings. He made some appointments and visited the landlords. Some places were holes in the wall. Some were in areas that made him nervous. Some didn't smell right. Finally, he found one. It wasn't much, but it was clean.

"When things get better I'll find a new place," he thought.

The landlord lived downstairs with his elderly wife, and they seemed to be nice. Edwin put down one month's rent as a deposit and reported it to Ruth. He could move in January first.

"When will you be leaving the hospital?" Ruth asked.

"January first."

"Ugh! I'll talk with the Team."

A few days later she came back and confronted Edwin.

"It is in your best interest to leave the hospital before January first."

"Why?"

"Because on January first new rules go into effect for discharge, and you won't be able to get out of the hospital. You have an apartment and a job. You can stay at my place for a few days. You can be my guest!"

"OK. I'll leave December 23. I can't move my stuff in until the new year anyway."

"What stuff is that?"

"My parents held onto my furniture when I left the house."

"You have a rabbi! I'll see that we get the paperwork done before then."

So the paperwork was done, and Ruth took Edwin to her apartment and showed him around. It had a main floor and a basement as well.

"You can sleep on the couch for a few days. Do you like it?"

"The couch?"

She laughed.

"Yes, I do," he said and gave her a peck on the cheek.

"What was that for?"

"I'm thanking you."

She put her head against his chest and put her arms around him.

"I'll make blintzes," she said.

As for his employer, Edwin approached his supervisor faintly.

"I have to tell you something."

"What is it?"

"I have mental illness."

His supervisor was taken aback.

"Is it going to be a problem?"

"No."

"Then don't worry about it."

And Edwin returned to his duties hoping there would be no problems with the judge. He had spent two years in County Hospital.

Part 5 (of 8)

The Struggle to Succeed and the Resulting Relapse

Chapter 42: Edwin Moves In

Ruth was in the kitchen when her daughter Sarah walked in.

"What are you doing?" Sarah demanded.

"Making blintzes."

"I spent all day cleaning this apartment!"

"And a fine job you did, my balebosta, but we have to eat."

"Blintzes?"

"I want you to meet Edwin Potter. He's going to be staying here for a few days until he can move into his apartment. You might like him."

"Is he Jewish?"

"No. He's just been discharged from the hospital, and he's my guest."

"Your guest from the hospital?! We'll talk later."

And she went into another room.

"She'll be all right," said Ruth. "As for you, my father was a gentle man, and he taught me to look for the good in people. My mother was of a different persuasion."

There was a knock at the door, and Ruth let in a young woman.

"Oh, I'm glad you're here! I want to introduce you. This is Edwin Potter. He'll be living with us for a few days – "

Edwin waved.

"— and this is Trishara Cohen, my niece. She's a Court Recorder."

"Hello," she said, then, to Ruth, "Is Sarah here?"

"I'm here!" called Sarah. "I'm getting ready for work."

She came out, and the two of them started to talk. Sarah worked as a waitress. What was of interest to Edwin were Trishara's comments about her job.

"When I'm in Court I record everything as it goes by, but when I'm doing a transcript I do my best to make the judge and the prosecutor look good. I eliminate the umms and rewrite the bad sentences. And the Defendant I make look bad. I make him stutter and put in umms and things like that. I don't change the content, but the jury deliberates with this."

Ruth, hearing this, changed the subject.

"Edwin, you should write a book."

"I don't know how to write a book," he said, thinking about Trishara's words.

"Try! There is a need for it, and you're the only one who can do it."

And the two girls left the apartment.

"Sarah and my other three girls live in our house with their father. He always wanted a son, and I never gave him one. So he had an affair – and she gave him a son! It's all hush-hush. Then one day all of my jewelry disappeared! Manuel – that's him – said that someone probably came in and stole all of it – including my favorite necklace. He never filed a police report. Then one day I saw it on her. 'Oh, no, Ruth! You're imagining things. They were just costume jewelry. I'm sure that there are many identical necklaces.' And we've been arguing ever since about all of his charades. A plague on both of his houses! And the girls, of course, defend their father because they live with him, and he influences them. So we have the civil divorce. Now I want the Jewish divorce."

Sherry entered at that moment.

"I would divorce that man if we weren't divorced already! I just spent another hour arguing with him about the house! I'm going downstairs. If you hear an explosion that will be me going off. Hi, Edwin."

She went downstairs.

"What a crazy apartment this is!" cried Ruth. "I want to talk to you now while we have a moment's peace. Once you move into your apartment you should find a girlfriend of your own. How long were you in the hospital?"

"Four and a half years."

"That's enough time. You should find a younger woman – younger than me, that is. I'll see if Sarah will go out with you. She's a wonderful daughter."

So Ruth persuaded her daughter to go on a date – which went nowhere – and helped Edwin move his furniture and belongings into his new – well, clean – apartment on River Road in Southland.

Chapter 43: Probation's Follow-up

Edwin reported for his weekly Probation session as he was required to do. Louise Tolston followed up on what Judge Washington had told Edwin.

"We want you to inform people of your history and Court status. We want you to tell people what you did."

Edwin did a quick double-take. Then, while feigning a handshake with some invisible person, he said, "You mean like saying to one of the women at work, 'Hi, I'm Edwin Potter! Killed my wife. Beat my son. Say, I'd like to see you alone for a minute after the meeting.' Is that what you're telling me?"

There was silence. Edwin continued.

"And what are you going to be doing to help me to make this re-entry into society?"

"What do you mean?"

"I don't see any of you out there saying anything good about me. The Court, the news, and mystery writers are all out there giving me this bad press, and I'm supposed to walk out there like a babe in the woods and tell people that all is well now. Do you think – in all Creation – that this is really going to work?"

"Your case is different."

Edwin kept his mouth shut and gave her a stern look.

Chapter 44: Sasha's Fear

It was early Spring – about Easter time – when Sasha decided to have Easter dinner at her home. It was a cape cod with not much room for relatives and a growing family, but she managed. Richard was now about two and a half years old, and his younger brother Peter was about one and a half.

Edwin was still a loner. Rather than being with family in the dining room where it was too crowded for his tastes, he was in the living room reading a magazine. He looked up when Sasha walked in.

"You know, you could be with the rest of us in the other room."

"Don't talk to me that way," he said out of character.

She fell to the floor.

"I have two young boys. Please don't hurt me!"

Edwin moaned, "Give me a break!" and headed out to the dining room.

Chapter 45: Meet Myra Agnello

Having established himself at work and in the community, Edwin was approached by Ruth in the early spring.

"You should go to one of the churches in the area that hold a singles' night. There is a popular one up the road a piece."

"Did you ever go?"

"None of your business!" she said with a laugh. "My daughters are trying to fix me up with a blind date. So go. I'll tell you all about it."

So that Friday evening Edwin, with an address from Ruth, went to a singles' night. The format was that there would be refreshments followed by announcements followed by group discussion topics. The object was to break the ice and get people to talk with each other. Then they would split up and continue their conversations more intimately.

Apparently Edwin had chosen the wrong topic. After fending off questions like, "Are you an ax murderer?" there was no woman in the group who enticed him. When the group broke up, he wandered the room, making a moderate show of mingling just like everyone else. There were a few failed attempts at making conversation until one slim blonde made her way over to him.

"Hello," she said. "My name is Myra."

"I'm Edwin."

"I'm an ICU nurse supervisor at a general hospital."

"I'm an engineer."

"It's interesting how engineers and nurses wind up together. Do you have children?" Before Edwin could answer, "Wait! Let me try something. Hold out your hand… No, the other one. I'm going to read your palm. It's a party trick that I read about."

Edwin listened with interest.

"This is the hand that tells us how things are today. Let's see… This line says that you have one child, and it's a boy. I have two girls both under ten. And – ooh! Look at this! This is your head line, and it's broken right in half as though something happened to your mind. Huh!"

And she continued on, not realizing just how close she was to the truth. Then she grabbed his pinky by the tip and shook it.

"And this little piggy is crooked. It probably means that you're a murderer," she said with a smile.

Edwin only listened.

"It's getting late," said Edwin. "Could we meet again?"

"All right. I'll give you my phone number."

And she did. And he gave her his. No last names. No addresses. He supposed that it was a good rule overall.

Chapter 46: Ruth's Blind Date

A few days after meeting Myra, Edwin talked with Ruth.
"So how did your blind date go?"

"Ugh! He should live so long! He showed up with a suitcase!"

"A suitcase!?"

"I told him that I was not going to spend my evening with a man who has no respect for me. He said that everybody 'does it' these days. I told him that he would have to leave. And we went back and forth. I felt like I was arguing with a patient. Finally! After all of that he left. It took half an hour to get him to realize that I was serious. A few more minutes and I would have called the police."

Edwin had never heard of such a thing.

Chapter 47: Edwin Leaves NLO

Edwin had found some answers to his research project at work. He approached the Research and Development Director.

"I was reading through the literature on thin-film resistor breakdown, and what I found is that the problem arises when the resistor values are adjusted by rubbing them manually. It creates a hollow –"

The Director started to listen.

"—and the breakdown occurs in the thinner area."

The Director started to fume.

"What needs to be done is to develop a machine to rub the resistors evenly."

The Director was enraged.

"NO! NO! YOU ARE WRONG! YOU DO NOT KNOW WHAT YOU ARE DOING! YOU ARE OFF THE PROJECT!"

Edwin felt embarrassed and guilty for being such a schmuck. He felt that this must be one of the people who is smarter than him as his mother had always said.

So Edwin went back to his regular engineering design duties. In a few days he saw the Director again with a young woman in tow who held pad and pen at the ready to record his every word.

Being generally discouraged, unhappy overall by the lack of professional challenge, and looking for that Holy Grail of job hopping – higher income that want ads advertised and his peers were receiving – he decided to look for a new job.

Chapter 48: First Date

Edwin had called Myra for a date, and she agreed, offering to meet him at her house. When he arrived, she invited him in and to have a seat. Something didn't seem right, though.

"I have something to ask you. You're mentally ill, aren't you?"

Edwin couldn't imagine how to avoid the question. Ruth's advice didn't seem to fit with direct questioning.

"Yes," he answered. How did she figure this one out?

"I thought so. And your wife didn't die in a car accident, did she?"

"No, she didn't."

How could he get out of this?

"How did she die?"

Edwin choked.

"I – she – she died at my hands," he answered, waiting for the worst.

"What else did you tell me that isn't true?"

"That's it. I'm an engineer. I have a job. I have a bachelor's degree --."

"Oh!" she exclaimed with a jerk of her head. "I didn't expect that. Are you okay?"

"My illness is in full remission."

"There was something about you that said you have mental illness. I sent my two girls out tonight with their father because I didn't know what you were going to do after I asked you about it. But I kept the date with you because I told myself, 'People get well.' Are you taking medication?"

"No. The doctor doesn't see the need for it."

"Huh! My father died when I was young. He had a heart attack, and my mother didn't do anything about it. She thought he was going to be all right. Maybe that's why I became a nurse.

"My ex-husband, Joseph, is a chemist, but he got laid off recently. He never really liked his job, so he's working at the local wine shop. He loves it, but it cut his child support payments 'way back. And it's hurting the kids. They're with him now, but they live with me.

"He's hard to get along with. He taped a quotation to the refrigerator, 'Those who ignore the past are condemned to repeat it.' And he has all of his crap in the basement. It's filled to the ceiling! I keep asking him to clean it out, but he never does.

"Do you go to church?"

"No, I don't," said Edwin.

"I'm what they call 'spiritual but not religious.' I don't know if there is a God, but I have my moments. I was in ICU just last week, and we had an old woman intubated and lying in the bed, waiting to die. Then all of a sudden she sat up, looked around calling, 'Jesus? Jesus?' Then she fell back dead. It took me five minutes to pull myself back together again."

"How about your mother?" asked Edwin.

"It's good that you ask that question. She's doing well. She lives alone in Seattle. She's in her seventies. I'm her only child. She started late. I worry about her. She has no one to take care of her, and the city has the highest suicide rate in the country because of all of the rainy weather. Where do you work?"

"I work for a place called NLO. They make parts for radios, but I'm looking for a new job. They don't treat me right over there."

Myra looked concerned.

"I'm concerned about your job-hopping. How long were you there?"

"About ten months."

"And what about before that?"

"I was in the hospital for about four and a half years."

"Do you play an instrument?"

"I strum a little guitar. Why?"

"I have a cousin who's a hit in Nashville."

"Really?"

"I'll play one of his albums for you someday. Where do you live?"

"I have an apartment in Southland."

"I want to see it."

Edwin hesitated.

"OK. When?"

"Well, not right now. We can talk about that. Let's have dinner first. I have a live lobster that I can throw in the pot, and Joe, despite all of the complaints that I have about him, taught me to taste and appreciate wine. How does that sound to you?"

"It's all new to me. Let's do it!"

So Edwin sat at the table while Myra prepared the meal, and they conversed.

"Do you visit your son?"

"I see him on weekends, but I have to be supervised. The judge just denied permission for me to see him alone."

"Oh, that's rough. My two girls live with me. They're young yet, and I worry about them. Gloria is the younger one. I had to stay on bed rest when I was carrying her. She's a happy child, but she has her moments. I bought a rabbit for her, and she doesn't like it. And I don't know why. It bothers me. Randi is just like her father – never happy with what she has. Do you like any movies?"

"I like action-adventure, but I prefer ones with a plot. Star Wars was good."

"I didn't like those."

And they chatted away while the dinner cooked. It didn't take long. Then they ate, enjoyed some wine, and then the night was over.

"I have to say – even in this short time – that you amaze me. I never heard of anyone coming so far after having such an illness. Let's get together next weekend."

"I see Denny on weekends."

"All weekend?"

"No, but I also have to do my laundry and shopping."

She looked at him intently.

"You make time for what is important to you. Call me. Good night."

Chapter 49: Rabbits and Fathers

The next time that Edwin saw Myra was at her home, and her two girls were with her. It was time to break the ice with them. Just like Myra said, Randi was a stormy personality, never happy.

"Hi, Randi," he said in a friendly fashion.

She ignored him and walked away. Myra started after her.

"I think the problem," he said to Myra, "is that she thinks I am here to replace her father. I think it will have to be up to you to tell her that is not the story."

Myra chased after Randi, and Edwin overheard.

"That was rude what you did, but maybe I can help you. Edwin is not here to replace your father. What you have with your father is something special, and I don't want to break that up. But I need my friends, too."

Myra came back.

"She's thinking now."

"What about Gloria?"

"She is with her rabbit. She feeds it and takes care of it because she is kind, but she just doesn't like it."

So Edwin went in to see Gloria who was in the kitchen.

"Hi," he said – his standard opening. "I see that you have a rabbit."

"I don't like him."

"I can see that you take good care of him. His coat is nice. His nose wiggles. Why don't you like him?"

She shrugged.

"Is he the wrong color?"

She shook her head no.

"Is he too little?"

"I don't like his ears."

Edwin didn't think that he would get this far.

"What's wrong with his ears?"

"They don't stand up."

Poor rabbit. His ears lay down.

"I'm sorry to hear that."

Myra overheard the whole thing and looked hurt.

"What am I going to do?"

"I guess you're going to have to choose between selling him or making a stew."

"Sometimes children are hard to love."

Chapter 50: Clinic for Mental Health

Edwin faced Doctor Howard Simon, the psychologist from the Midland County Clinic for Mental Health.

"You've been out of the hospital for a few months now. How is everything going? How is work?"

"I changed jobs."

"Why?"

"I didn't like the way they were treating me." He explained about the research project.

"Also they did not allow me to play on the company volleyball team. After they lost their game, I told them that I had been on the championship intramural volleyball team at college."

"What happened then?"

"They walked away."

"Look into my eyes," said the doctor, "and don't look away."

Edwin looked. And looked again. And looked some more.

"Is there a point to this?" asked Edwin.

"Maybe not," said the doctor, breaking his gaze.

"Staring into the eyes of a killer until he can bear the weight of his sins no longer?"

"So where are you working now?"

"Coast Radio. They're a global communication company. The pay is better, too."

"Anything else?"

"I have a girlfriend."

"Maybe you can talk with Ronnie Kenwood about that. He's a social worker. This is the last session that you and I will be having. I've been assigned other duties. You will meet with him here at the same time and place. Good luck to you."

Chapter 51: Review Hearing

Judge Washington spoke.
"Would you enter your appearances for the record."
"Patsy Arpin for the State."
Apparently Georgia Bailey had moved on to other things.
"Daniel Aaron for the Co-mmittee, Edwin Potter."
"Mr. Aaron, I have a Motion from you on behalf of your client to allow him unsupervised visits with his son. How old is the child now?"
"We have the grandparents here, Your Honor, who can give a better answer."
"Mrs. Potter -- ?"
"He is about seven years old now."
"And how have the visits been going? Does Edwin Potter show up?"
"Yes, Your Honor. He is there at every opportunity."
"Have there been any problems?"
"No, Your Honor. He is a good father to his son."
"Prosecutor?"
"No problems, Your Honor."
"Mrs. Potter, what kind of activities do they engage in?"

"They wrestle. They color and paint. He reads stories. Sometimes my husband will take them on an outing for ice cream."

The judge pondered.

"Prosecutor, do you have anything to say?"

"The State would proffer, Your Honor, that although on the surface Mr. Potter seems to be in control of himself, he is still a menace to society. There is dark history in other, similar cases where the Co-mmittee lost control of himself within only a few days of his release."

"But not in this case."

"No, Your Honor. The State wants to make clear that the child was also a victim of the actions taken by Mr. Potter on that night now five years ago."

The judge pondered.

"For the record, how long has Mr. Potter been out?"

"About six months."

"Mr. Potter, are you employed now?"

"Yes, Your Honor."

"Continuously?"

"Yes."

There was silence.

"I am going to deny your Motion, Mr. Aaron, without prejudice, and I will continue the present Order. You may apply again in the future if the situation warrants."

Chapter 52: Crystal Radio

Short and sweet, Edwin did not like Coast Radio, either. After a judge's decision to break up AT&T, the communication industry de-stabilized, and Edwin looked for another place to go. Myra was supportive. So he joined a place called Crystal Radio which was a small manufacturer who made parts for commercial and military radios. He was assigned to Special Assemblies and thought that he would be happy there.

It was at this time that Edwin decided to sell his house which he still otherwise owned since the incident, move out of River Road, buy a new townhouse further out west from Southland in Bloom, and take the train to work every day. There was no objection from Louise Tolston, so he did.

One day at work his boss came to him and said that there was someone there from the government who wanted to speak with him about his military clearance.

"It's good to see you working," said the man. "I'm just here to check where you've been since you left your employer six years ago. We know you were in the hospital for four and a half years. Where did you go then?"

Edwin told him.

"Did you leave the country at all?"

"No."

It was a short visit, and he passed the interview pending the follow-up.

When he got back to his desk he found the owner of the company hanging a chart on the wall. It showed the increase in the number of defective parts over recent time.

"When I find the person responsible for this, I'm going to fire him! This is costing us money and customers!"

Edwin returned to his desk feeling guilty. He knew from his youth that his parents' anger was his fault, and this was no different. Yet he was professional enough to return to his work and, in this case, design the next radio component.

When he finished the design package, he gave it to the Special Assemblies production supervisor who then assigned it to an assembler. In a few hours he had a component ready for test – and the test failed. He spoke with the assembler, Celeste, who said the directions were poor. So he gave the design package – unchanged – back to the supervisor to assign it to someone else. In a few hours he had another component ready for test, and this one was good. One more time he asked the supervisor to assign the package to someone else who had not yet worked on it, and the results were good again. He pulled the supervisor aside and spoke quietly.

"I found the person who is causing the defects," he said nervously. "Celeste."

"No, not my people!"

"Yes. She said the instructions were no good, and that is why I asked you to take the package as is and give it some other assemblers. They could build it, but she could not."

The supervisor looked terrified.

"You had better train her or something real fast before somebody else finds out."

And he left her to go to his desk where the phone was ringing. He answered it, and it was his old boss from Coast Radio calling him to see if he would come back to work with them.

"How did you find me?" asked Edwin.

"You left your new employer name and address with personnel. I took a chance."

"Any pay increase?"

"Well, you gained some experience. I guess that we can give you something for that. Will you take the offer?"

Edwin thought. Maybe the work world wasn't so perfect. Maybe Coast Radio wasn't so bad.

"Okay. I'll turn in my resignation and start in two weeks."

"Fine. I'll make the preparations. Thank you, and good luck."

Edwin hung up the phone and then called Myra, telling her that he wanted to see her that night. She agreed. When he got there he popped the question.

"Will you marry me?"

To which she happily answered yes. And they smooched, much to the disgust of her two girls.

"I would have your child," she breathed, "But I would have to be on bed rest like I was with Gloria."

This thought made Edwin nervous. Would she die otherwise? But she had done it before, but he was still nervous.

"Tomorrow night we'll pick out a ring."

Chapter 53: Ruth's Comments

Edwin walked into Ruth's apartment to tell her the good news. Sherry was there as well.

"Manuel died," said Ruth.

Edwin held back with his news.

"And I had to sit shiva with his girlfriend and son there – wearing my necklace! You're only supposed to say good about the deceased, so I kept my mouth shut for the entire time. 'She's grieving,' they said"

"I'm sorry for your anguish," said Edwin.

With a pause, Ruth asked, "What's new with you?"

"I'm getting married," he proclaimed softly.

"Oh! Mazel Tov! Congratulations!"

"Congratulations!" added Sherry. "That's wonderful!"

"The ceremony will be in about a year."

"She's too old for you." said Ruth.

"Ruth, let him make his own decisions if he is going to be the head of a family."

"She is too old for you! Her friends say she is over forty. You're only what – thirty-five?"

"Thirty-one."

"All the worse."

"I'm not going to stay and listen to this. Let him make his own decisions," said Sherry, and she went downstairs.

"Myra is only three years older than me --."

"So she says."

"Who cares? What about the eighteen years of difference between you and me? And our friendship? She is thirty-four."

"I don't like her."

"She doesn't like you, either."

Ruth grunted.

"Listen to me. She isn't smart enough for you! Is that what you want?"

That one resonated with him. He did not know what to say, but the seed was now planted. And he thought. His inner voice took him back to his family, "Do as you are told! Other people know more than you do."

"My head hurts," said Ruth, holding her head. She lit a cigarette.

Chapter 54: Learning About Each Other

Times with Myra were wonderful, and they got better with every meeting between them. Myra came to visit him in his townhouse in Bloom, and he met her mother who was happy about the engagement. They both bought new cars, Edwin having the money now to replace the car that his father had given to him. They went for rides together on the country roads where Myra lived. And they cleaned out her basement – following the letter of notification to her ex – filling a forty-five cubic yard dumpster to the brim in the process.

At work Edwin felt like he was getting nowhere, so he signed up for a master's degree program at State University. Myra supported him. Daniel Aaron – still part of the picture – asked that Edwin forward copies of his report cards to him. And at the review hearing six months later Judge Washington allowed Edwin to visit his son unsupervised.

At this time Edwin also rented an apartment in West Southland to be closer to work, to Myra, and to his reporting officers. Myra liked it too and came to visit occasionally. But he did not sell the townhouse. He rented that out to a minister and his family.

But Edwin, too, was hard to love as Myra had said about her children. He felt uncomfortable with Myra. Ruth's words still stayed with him, and eventually he broke off the engagement.

Chapter 55: Meet Lucinda

Edwin surrounded himself with a stormy silence and stayed away from Ruth. Unperturbed, she called him on the telephone, angering him even further. Sometimes he would hang up or not even answer. She told him that he did the right thing. Because she had helped him through his trials and fought for him, though, he believed her.

After the storm abated her suggestion was to look through the personal ads in the newspaper which he did. It was a challenge with each woman having a laundry list of expectations to qualify him for a first date. Finally, he came across Lucinda Tanzer who sent him a letter with a photo of her enclosed.

They met, and at Christmas they spent the night together. Soon she broke the news to him that she was pregnant. He proposed marriage – happy with the thought of having a child – and she accepted. He told her of his illness and involvement with the Court. She vowed to stay with him and invited him to meet her family.

Her father was a Korean War veteran who still had nightmares. The story went that the Koreans would come into camp at night and cut the throats of all of the soldiers except one who would live to tell the tale. He was the one.

Her uncle built a house in the middle of nowhere and wanted to sell it to Edwin as an investment.

"What am I going to do with it way out here?" asked Edwin.

Nevertheless, Edwin was happy, and he and Lucinda planned to marry in March. Her parents were glad, too, that this time the man would marry her. Then they heard his story from her and wondered if this really was going to be a good thing.

"I hope you know what you're doing," said her mother. "Does he have a job?"

"He's an engineer."

"But does he have a job?"

"He said he works for Coast Radio, and he's pursuing his master's degree."

"I never heard of such a thing for someone with all of his problems. Well, you have to believe in people. I wish you two the best of luck. You'll need it."

Edwin's own family was silent other than a brief congratulation.

Prior to the wedding, Lucinda filed for bankruptcy so that Edwin would not become responsible for her debts. Her landlady, having not been paid her rent, was happy to see her go. Lucinda's old car was in need of repairs, and Edwin paid for those. And, to tie all of it up neatly, Ruth was the "best man."

In September their child Cheryl was born much to Edwin's joy. At the hospital he spent his time holding the tiny hand of his new daughter.

"Most men don't spend nearly that amount of time with their child," said a nurse.

Edwin and Lucinda had set up housekeeping in West Southland, and in a few months Sherry and Ruth came to visit. Ruth, having experience as a public health nurse, showed Lucinda how to give Cheryl a bath without dropping her onto the floor. Then Lucinda put the baby to bed. As the three others talked in the living room, Lucinda came out naked holding only a towel in front of her. There was silence as everyone looked.

"I'm a free spirit," she said.

There was still silence.

"Oh!" said someone.

Chapter 56: Early Home Life

Lucinda "liked to work" but decided to stay home with Cheryl for some months while the baby was so young. She and Edwin decided not to put her into day care right away because, first, they wanted to be with her. Second, they thought she was too young.

Chapter 57: Ophthalmic Scanning

At school Edwin had started a master's project: ophthalmic scanning. But being married now, with a child, and with a long drive several times per week, he gave up his quest and told his mentor who asked him to write a paper.

The idea of the project was to improve the ultrasound scanning of the eye. Currently it was being done with a piezoelectric device being mechanically waved back and forth in front of the eye. Edwin saw their idea as archaic in this day and age.

"There's got to be a better way," he told himself.

So he suggested a phased-array device with digital signal processing based upon a priori information. His mentor was eternally grateful, and Edwin got an "S" on his report card for his effort. And he withdrew from the master's program. Only many years later did he ask himself if his idea would have qualified for a patent.

Chapter 58: The Struggle Begins

After some time passed, Lucinda was back at work, but there were problems at work for Edwin. A junk bond investor got a hold of Coast Radio and sold off all of its assets. His department was one of them, and his boss called him in to tell Edwin that he was being laid off.

Lucinda now was the sole provider for the household while Edwin received unemployment benefits and took care of the baby while looking for a new job. After three months an outplacement service was able to find him a position with Storm Utility. Max Wilson – a fellow alumnus to Edwin – and Joseph Nelson hired Edwin, and he was to start at the very beginning of January. Some of his fellow employees from Coast Radio who had jumped ship earlier were there already.

Edwin, having told the good news to Lucinda, wanted to start a master's program right away, so he sat down with Lucinda to discuss it.

"I'm not going to be able to help you much around the apartment because I will be studying. Occasionally I may come up for air, but most of the work is going to be on your shoulders. We will benefit in the long run, but it is going to be hard at this time. Is there anything that you want to say?"

"OK."

So Edwin began his master's program at his alma mater.

Still, there were problems. Supportive of him to the point of going to battle, Lucinda argued with their landlady. So Edwin decided that the best thing to do was to buy a home for his family. He sold his townhouse, bought a small cape cod in Southland, and moved out of West Southland with Lucinda and Cheryl. He also bought a new car for Lucinda as her old clunker had reached the end of its natural life.

And before the end of the year was out, Sasha had had another baby boy who she named Ian Cisco. And it was about this time that she and Larry decided to move out of Southland (for that was where they were) and into Pennsylvania, much to the chagrin of the remainder of the family.

Two years passed at work, and Edwin received a promotion to Engineer A. And in a few more months he received his master's degree.

And Cheryl was growing up. Edwin and Lucinda were in in bed asleep one early morning, and Edwin was awakened in an instant from the sound of the bedroom door being opened. He could see the top of a little head making her way to her mother. Then all of a sudden she smacked her mother in the head, waking her in terror with the comment, "Mommy, sun's up!"

And the other good news was that Sherry was engaged to be married the following year.

But not everything was beautiful. The feminist movement was becoming a viable force, and workplaces everywhere were becoming battlegrounds. Edwin was approached by an older woman in the office who had borne and raised ten respectable children. She praised him for his professionalism and maturity but also warned him that there were several women in the office – unnamed – who were "out to get him."

Joseph Nelson was developing into a difficult person. Although he was seemingly caring and soft-spoken when Edwin joined Storm Utility, Edwin was beginning to see his darker side. Edwin had made some significant cost-saving moves on the projects that he inherited – about one million dollars – and he had asked if there would be any bonus money for him that year.

"Bonus?" asked Nelson. "There is no bonus for that for you. That is what you were hired to do."

At the Clinic things were better. Six years had passed since Edwin was released from County Hospital. Ronnie Kenwood was going to pull some strings to see if he could help Edwin get his case dismissed. Soon there was an appointment for him to be interviewed by two psychologists from the Clinic, and he did very well. A report was submitted to the judge recommending that his case be dismissed, but three days later a second report was submitted that told frightful tales about Edwin. This was intended to reverse the earlier recommendation for dismissal.

"Tell me, doctor," began Daniel Aaron, "how many times did you personally examine Mr. Potter?"

"Once."

"And yet you wrote two reports."

There was no response from the Doctor.

"Did you write two reports, Doctor?"

"Yes! I did!"

"And did you find in your examination, Doctor, that Mr. Potter just recently received his Master's degree in Engineering?"

"He only thinks he received his master's degree!"

"I assure you, Doctor, that he received it. I have copies of the reports from the University."

Although Daniel Aaron made his arguments about bias and discrimination, the judge did not dismiss the case.

At home Lucinda was appalled and blamed the decision on Edwin rather than the prejudices that exist in society against the mentally ill.

"You are an embarrassment to me!" she cried.

"An embarrassment to you? You had nothing when I met you! You were in debt. You had no money!" he roared.

"You're just a fart in a gale of wind!"

"I bought you this house with the money that I had saved because you couldn't get along with the landlady!!"

Lucinda responded in a rage, roaring without any hint of sense. Cheryl was terrified and hid under the kitchen table.

"You're scaring Cheryl!" he declared and pulled her out and picked her up.

Lucinda stopped.

On another matter, Ruth had moved out of her apartment and moved in with her now-married daughter Sarah in Virginia because she did not like the way the hospital was treating the patients. She spoke on the phone with Edwin.

"It's all about money," she said.

She was also continuing to have pains in the head. She found that it was a tumor and stopped smoking cigarettes but confided to Edwin that she thought it was too late.

Edwin, too, confided in her that he did not know where he was going.

"Wherever it is," she said supportively, "I'm sure you'll make it... Here. I want to give you a telephone number. My attorney gave it to me when I was having trouble with the judge in my divorce. He told me never to use his name."

She gave Edwin the number and then turned to another topic.

"Have you started writing your book?"

"No."

"Don't forget."

Chapter 59: Edwin Joins a Group

Edwin was diffident. People walked all over him. He was depressed at work and at all of the jobs he ever held. He did not believe that he was good enough to be a part of the picture. He believed that his co-workers were all better than he – Why else would they talk to him like they were his superiors? Thoughts of suicide were starting to bother him again.

But there was an ad in the paper about a group called the High-IQ Society. Edwin thought that he would give it a shot – having nothing to lose – and mailed in his SAT scores. A few weeks later he received a congratulatory letter: He had qualified for membership. He had to stop and think about that. Instead of being at the bottom of the heap he was in the top two percent. He sent the check and at the beginning of September received a new member kit and a membership certificate which he made a copy of – with the phone number – and hung in his office at work.

Over the cubicle wall at work he heard some women talking.

"If he can do it, so can I!"

A few weeks later he heard the same women talking over the wall.

"I failed the test."

"I'm sure it was discriminatory. There was probably a man giving the test."

"No, a woman gave the test, and another woman designed the test. I called her up. She said that I did not score high enough to qualify."

Edwin felt good. It was a few months after that when he received his promotion to Engineer, three years since joining the Company.

Chapter 60: Marriage Counseling

Things were not getting any better between Edwin and Lucinda. She raged; he could barely control himself because she knew how to push his buttons. Finally, as a desperate man he thought that he could put his therapy sessions to some good use. He asked Kenwood to perform some marriage counseling which was agreed to.

So at the next session all three of them took their seats in the office.

"What seems to be the problem?" asked Kenwood.

"We have a problem communicating," said Edwin.

"A problem communicating? Well, well!" said Kenwood with a laugh.

"I'm looking to you to help us through this."

"Me?" Ronnie said with another laugh.

Lucinda began to catch on, playing Edwin as the fool.

"If we can't resolve this, I'm going to file for divorce."

"Oh, divorce!"

More laughter.

"That's it! That's it!" roared Edwin. "I'm filing for divorce!"

And they packed up and left the social worker. During the drive Edwin calmed down.

"I want this to work," he said.

Lucinda was silent.

A few days later Lucinda didn't come home, and Cheryl didn't either. Edwin was nervous. It was pointless to call the police. They would say she was off on a trip and didn't tell him. Or they would accuse him of some dastardly plot and arrest him.

A day later he was looking through the drawers, and he found that his credit account had been forged to the tune of fifteen thousand dollars.

At the end of a week on a hot July night the phone rang. It was Lucinda.

"I want to come back," she said.

"I don't want you back."

"What about your daughter?"

"You can send her back."

Anger.

"Where did you go?" asked Edwin.

"I went to Cancun with a friend."

"You took Cheryl with you?"

"Yes."

"Where did you get the money from?"

"None of your business."

"We have nothing else to talk about. Good-bye."

And he hung up.

The next night Edwin received a call from Daniel Aaron.

"I have bad news for you. Lucinda filed a Domestic Violence complaint against you. The police are coming to remove you from the house. They will give you ten minutes to pack and leave. I'm giving you a heads-up. We'll talk about it later."

Aaron hung up.

Edwin thought quickly. What is this argument going to be about? Money. So he quickly packed the financial records and bills, his toiletries, his clothes and got it all done and into the car just as the police arrived. They were very cautious, probably informed of a Domestic Violence dispute which can be deadly and Edwin's rap sheet.

Where could he go? His parents. Maybe they could suggest something.

"You can't stay here," they said. "Denny lives here, and the Court won't allow the two of you to live in the same house. You'll have to live someplace else, maybe the YMCA."

So that is where Edwin went.

At work the next day Edwin received a call from Lucinda.

"It was the only thing that I could think of to get back into the house."

The next day he spoke with Aaron.

"I want a divorce."

"Remember that you have a Domestic Violence complaint against you. Did you do anything to warrant that?"

"Nothing. She said she had gone to Cancun with a friend – probably a boyfriend – and Cheryl. I wouldn't take her back. She called me at work today and told me that was the only way she could think of to get back into the house."

There was silence.

"All right..."

"I want the divorce. I can see what my future is going to be with this woman. Every time I do something that she is not happy with she is going to have me arrested. And I want nothing in common with her," he finished, remembering the problems of Sherry and Ruth.

"Where are you living now?"

"At a YMCA – listening to people scream in the middle of the night. I guess this is supposed to be my place in society."

"Technically you're homeless... All right, Edwin. I'll see what I can do, but let it go for a while. Maybe things will clear up."

Chapter 61: Marriage and Divorce

It was August. The year had passed now where Sherry was to be married, and she made a beautiful bride. Edwin – and Ruth – had been invited to the wedding, but Edwin broke the news that he and Lucinda were going to be divorced. Having said that, they all ignored it and went on to have a good time for the evening.

At the Clinic Edwin had a new social worker, a woman by the name of Barbra Vogel. At their first session he gave her a hug, and then they went on about their business. After a few more weeks of hugs, she threw him out of the Clinic. It took a few minutes of talking to himself before he realized that he was on his own. No judge. No doctor. Just him and the Probation Officer Louise Tolston. Life was good.

In September Aaron, now old and frail, thought that he had waited long enough for the discord between Edwin and Lucinda to resolve itself. With the dissension still persisting, Aaron filed for the divorce with a comment to Edwin.

"On the other matter, Judge Washington has retired, so we will have to wait until another judge is assigned before we can inform the Court. I have in mind another attorney – very good – who will take up your case."

In January there was to be an appearance before a judge of the Family Court just to set things into motion. That day Aaron gave Edwin his keys and asked him to park the car while he started off in his infirmity down the block to the Courthouse.

The Court's decision was to have Edwin live on his own and pay his own expenses as well as to pay for the house and the utility bills pending a later decision on child support. His opposing argument was that Lucinda had a job and could afford to pay some of her own expenses, but that was denied. These were hard times for him.

There was also to be an evaluation of the relationship between him and his daughter. This was to be done at a local library. So for several weeks the evaluator met with Edwin and Cheryl. Father and daughter rolled on the rug and wrestled with each other. They played games and read together. Edwin also at times brought in coloring books and watercolors. When it was time to go back to Court, the report was very good and in Edwin's favor, and he was allowed to see Cheryl unsupervised.

In late March Edwin moved out of the YMCA and moved in with a stranger, Ken O'Keefe, to share his apartment in Parkerton as a cost-saving measure as well as having a nicer place to live.

Having been saddled with the heating bills, Edwin examined them every month and saw that they were high. He racked his brains as to why until it occurred to him that Lucinda must have had a window open all winter. So he got into his car and drove over there for a look, and, sure enough, there was a window open wide on the second floor. He parked, got out of the car, walked up to the door, and rang the bell as a man came out with a change of clothes over his arm, got into a car and drove away.

Lucinda came to the door angrily, but Edwin stated his case. She shut the door on him, but having said what he needed to say, Edwin went back to the apartment.

That night there was a knock at the door. When Edwin answered, there was a Parkerton police officer there with a warrant for Edwin's arrest. Edwin called up the stairs to Ken while he was being handcuffed, and then he was led off to the police station.

Chapter 62: Bail

The phone rang, and Derek Potter answered it.

"Dad, it's Edwin."

"Yes?"

"I'm at the Parkerton police station."

"What happened? What's wrong?" he said anxiously.

"Lucinda had me arrested."

"For what?"

"I can't go into that now. I'm on the station phone. I need bail money so that I can go back to work in the morning."

"Bail money! How much?"

"They'll take five hundred dollars – cash. That's ten percent of the full amount. If we can swing this, you can take me home, and I'll write you a check to cover it."

"All right. I'll see what I can do. You might have to spend the night there."

And they hung up.

"Ellen!" Derek called. "Edwin was arrested! I need five hundred dollars cash for bail money!"

"I don't have that! You'll have to go to one of those bail bond offices. You'd better hurry. They might be closing soon."

So Derek made some calls and found an office that would be open until ten. He drove over and got the money, then went to the police station to spring Edwin who told him what happened.

"You know," said Derek, "if your bride has any sense she would realize that if she puts you in jail she is going to have to pay her own bills."

With that Derek drove Edwin back to the apartment where Ken met them at the door, asking them if they needed any money to which they answered "no" but thanked him anyway.

In a few days Edwin appeared before the Family Court judge with Daniel Aaron and Lucinda with her attorney. Aaron explained the story to the judge, and Lucinda dropped the complaint.

After the appearance Aaron took Edwin aside and whispered that he should not be making inspections of the home.

Chapter 63: Discipline at Work

There was a re-organization at work, and Edwin was able to get himself a new boss, one who through the grape vine was said to be headed for an executive position. His name was Matthew Hansen. Edwin could prove his own mettle, but he wanted to be certain to hang onto this man's coattails.

But there was a trouble-maker already making herself known to Hansen: Debbie Li. She claimed that someone was sabotaging her work in the Company and hinted in Edwin's direction.

Finally, Hansen had heard enough of it and called both of them into his office. Debbie stuck to her story. Edwin, who had been in his office writing a specification, detected some romantic overtones from Debbie and made it very clear that he had no interest in her.

"That's it!" said Hansen. "I'm giving both of you a verbal warning. The next step, if you continue, is a written warning. After that comes dismissal. Go back to work."

After Debbie left, Edwin took the bull by the horns.

"I was in my office writing a specification, and you know it."

With that he left.

Chapter 64: Research

It was May, and Edwin needed a break, a new relationship. So he went back to the Friday night church socials to look for a new friend, and he found someone interesting. Her name was Luella Kirchganger, and she was from Germany. She was a research scientist with a Ph.D. in pharmacology and worked for Big Pharma. Her English was not fluent, and she had a hard time saying it. She was looking for a cure for schizophrenia. Edwin commented that it was "interesting," and they decided to spend some time together.

There were some concerts in the park near to where she lived, so she packed a picnic basket, and they attended some of them. They had fun. Eventually she began to trust him and so invited him to her townhouse where they had long conversations about life, people and children.

One day they decided to meet in a parking lot to go to the mall. Edwin stood by while she sat in her car with the window down, and The Subject came up.

"Do you have schizophrenia in your family?"

"Yes," said Edwin, waiting to hear what would come next.

"Who?"

"My father's father."

Luella looked nervous.

"What about you?" she continued.

"Yes, I have schizophrenia. My first wife died as a result of it. I never got over it."

Luella looked terrified.

"I don't think this relationship has any future, but I need to ask you: Does it feel any different?"

Edwin thought.

"Yes, it does."

"Good-bye."

With that she roared out of the parking lot.

"Wait! I LOVE YOU!" cried Edwin as her car disappeared from sight. "Not that it matters..."

Everyone wants to help the mentally ill until she actually meets one.

Chapter 65: Try Again

Edwin pulled up to the curb outside the house as he was supposed to do in order to pick up his daughter for the visit. He saw that the window was still open on the second floor. And he thought about it. Cheryl had not come out five minutes after the scheduled pick-up time, and there was no word from Lucinda.

Finally, he could wait no more and went up to the front door and rang the bell. Lucinda came to the door, and Edwin pleaded nervously that the boiler would have to work harder to heat the house. She was risking a breakdown on a cold winter's night, and he had no money to have it fixed. Was Cheryl ready?

Lucinda went into a rage and disappeared into the house. When she came back she had something to say.

"I called the police! You better run!" and went back inside.

Edwin didn't feel like playing cops and robbers, so he walked slowly over to his car, grumbling all of the way, and leaned against it. In a minute the police pulled up and blocked him in the driveway.

"What's the problem?" asked one of the officers as he headed toward the house.

"She doesn't like me."

With that the two officers went inside. After a few minutes they came back out.

"Listen. Don't make trouble for us. I have to write a report on this, and I don't like writing reports. Stay out of each other's way!"

And they got into the squad car and left.

Lucinda called Edwin from the house.

"Cheryl is ready now."

Edwin waited.

"I was taking her to a child psychologist," she began.

"I hate psychologists," he said.

"He said that she shouldn't see you anymore because you're a bad influence on her. I told him to go to hell and get himself another sucker. Cheryl needs you."

Cheryl came out quietly and went to her father.

Edwin bent down.

"You are not the cause of the problems between Mommy and Daddy," he said.

Like her brother, she threw her arms around him and then held onto his ankle as he dragged her across the lawn.

"C'mon, Cheryl! You're going to ruin your clothes! I love you, too!"

They went out and had a good day. When they came back, the window on the second floor was closed. And Edwin gave Lucinda credit for not putting the child between their differences.

He told the tale to Louise Tolston the next time he went to report. Her pen was at the ready.

"I see that you're not writing any of this down," he said. "What are you doing? Waiting for the good part?"

"Nothing happened."

"That's right. Nothing happened."

She waited.

"Is there some guideline that says you cannot say good things about a Probationer? Another guy might have beaten her up or killed her and fled across state lines with the child. None of that happened."

And Louise began to write.

Chapter 66: Leon Rosenberg Takes Over

December had come again. Over a year had passed since Aaron filed for divorce, and he had become too sickly to carry on any further. Leon Rosenberg took over now on Aaron's recommendation. Leon was still a young man but helpful and knowledgeable about how people work.

"How is your son?"

"He's good. He's in high school now."

"How is he doing there?"

"He's above average."

"Do you still see him?"

"Birthdays and holidays," said Edwin uncomfortably. "I figure he needs his time to see friends and to do school projects and activities."

Leon was quiet for a moment.

"How about your daughter?"

"She is still in grammar school doing <u>very </u>well. She takes after me. I also play Monopoly with her. She lets me win, so she says."

"Do your parents attend the hearings?"

"No."

"Do you have anyone who you see?"

"There are some people who I met in the High-IQ Society. There are some regular monthly affairs that some of us attend. Once per month there is a dinner that we attend. This past month there was a guy there by the name of Frank Kirkland."

"Why? What's so special about him?

"I met him at State Hospital. He's a drug addict. Killed his father and wanted sex with me – or with any woman he could persuade. I kept my back to him all night."

"I guess he's trying to get back into the swing of things."

"My hope was that I wouldn't have to kill him to keep him off of me. Anyway, I let the Society hold a quarterly executive meeting in my apartment – with Ken's permission, of course. Girlfriends, no, although there was an interesting one from Germany with a Ph.D. who wants to find a cure for schizophrenia."

"How did that work out?"

"It ended before it started."

"All right," said Leon, changing the subject, "There is nothing that we can do now because we don't have a judge assigned to this case. I'll call the Court later this week to see if we can get a judge assigned. Just as a note, it seems that the Court lets your case fall through the cracks. The same is true for your criminal case as well. I'll be working on that one, too, with your permission."

"OK."

And that was pretty much the gist of their conversation. Edwin wrote him a check and spent his time at work and writing letters to Leon about Lucinda.

Chapter 67: The Newsletter

A few months passed. Edwin had been reading The Newsletter since he joined the High-IQ Society – or just "Society." It was the local venue for member expression and communication. There was a member who was greatly dissatisfied with all things, especially the Catholic Church, and he filled up the pages of The Newsletter every month with his diatribes.

Edwin was tired of it, so he wrote a letter to the Editor. Nothing changed, so he took the advice of a friend of the organization who he met at a Society party.

"If you don't like what you see, volunteer."

So with trepidation he began to write his own monthly column in the hope of changing the subject. He found that he liked the challenge, but he also found that his readers could be a critical bunch.

"It comes with the territory," he murmured to himself.

He also found that he needed to review English composition and grammar. He improved, but it was always an uphill struggle.

Shortly after this Lucinda found another man by the name of Wyatt Zucker and became pregnant with his child.

At this same time there was a national grant-writing contest held by the Society to benefit libraries. Edwin entered and tied with another member of the local group. Their grant was divided evenly and Edwin gave his share to the main Southland Library by the end of December.

Chapter 68: A Judge is Assigned

Three years later – three years! – after Aaron had filed for the divorce a judge was assigned to the case. Her name was Reanna Wood. All during this time Edwin had been taking care of himself with no judge, no doctor, and no therapist. And it was about this time that Daniel Aaron died. Rose, Aaron's secretary, had called Edwin and asked him to pick up his files, the remainder of them had already gone to Leon Rosenberg. Edwin went to the office, almost speechless. Daniel Aaron and Rose had done so much for him over the years, and now he was gone.

Judge Wood set a date for their appearances. Leon told Edwin that he should appear pro se as Lucinda was not going to have an attorney.

"She probably spent all of her money on men and vacations and can no longer afford an attorney," said Edwin.

So Edwin and Lucinda appeared before the judge. Lucinda was as pregnant as a house. Judge Wood glared at her. Lucinda made some weak arguments about why Edwin had disappointed her and deserved to be divorced from her, forgetting that it was he who had filed. She included the arguments that he did no work around her parents' house, that she would have to take care of the house and the baby while he was studying for his master's degree, and that he liked cookies. When Edwin's turn came, he said just a few words before the judge began to laugh at him. Edwin waited as the judge brought the day's proceedings to an end.

When he got home he sat in a chair and thought. Then he went through one of the bags he had packed for his stay and found the telephone number that Ruth had given to him and dialed it.

"Administrative Offices?"

He hesitated a moment. Then he began.

"I have a complaint about a judge. Where can I send a letter?"

Chapter 69: Nora Rodriguez

Half a year later in December Judge Wood declared that
Edwin and Lucinda were divorced. As Edwin had made the
mistake of putting Lucinda's name on the title to the house, he
had to remortgage the house in order to have her name
removed and achieve his goal of having nothing in common
with her. Things looked pretty iffy there as he now had child
support payments as a financial obligation to report. Even
Louise Tolston confided that in her experience the amount he
was assessed was high. But in March he was able to convince
the bank that he was good for the money, and the house was
his.

And Lucinda married Wyatt Zucker. In a few short
months she divorced him. Edwin looked for the third child.

There were changes at that time for Judge Wood as
well. She was moved from Family court to Criminal Court and
was assigned to Edwin's case. Leon Rosenberg was called by the
judge, and when she heard that Edwin had been without a
judge or – more important – psychiatric supervision for over
two years, she hit the ceiling. After the meeting was over Leon
confided to Edwin that she was going to put him back in State
Psychiatric Hospital and have him start all over again, but Leon
was able to convince her that he had done very well in all areas

during all of this time. The result was that Judge Wood ordered that he find a psychiatrist posthaste before she did put him in State.

So with help from his attorney Edwin found a forensic psychiatrist, Doctor Arthur Goodman, who was approved by the judge and began therapy immediately.

That was in February. Things had settled down by March, and Edwin thought to look for a girlfriend, somewhere... exotic. The Society bulletin had a personal ad listing from an international introductory service, so he tried that with the uncomfortable feeling of finding himself a mail order bride. A picture and a paragraph. They were all the same. How was one supposed to choose? Then a photo of a very beautiful Colombian woman, Nora Rodriguez, caught his eye. He felt that his chances were slim to none having his illness and not much money to speak of. Men from around the world would be offering her houses, boats, trips, cars, and so much more that he could not compete with.

"Oh, give her a thrill," he opined.

So he sat down and wrote a letter to her that expressed his deepest desire to talk with her. E-mail had not yet been invented.

In a few weeks, much to his surprise, there was a letter from her in his post office box with the same photo that he saw in the booklet.

"I received letters from men from all around the world who offered me houses, boats, trips, cars – but I believe that you are sincere."

And at forty years old, she at thirty-two, they began their long conversation, celebrating her birthday by phone the following July.

Chapter 70: License

With his divorce behind him and having a new friend to talk with, Edwin breathed a sigh of relief.

But not all was well in the department at Storm Utility. One of the secretaries, Golda, was openly critical of her boss who she saw as a sleaze.

"No more of that or I'll fire you," he warned.

"If you fire me you'll be on the six o'clock news – and I'm not kidding."

Office politics were played roughly in this big city department. The department head, Ted Fischer, never came out of his office to speak with any of the people who he was in charge of. Edwin tried to get out by looking for a new job somewhere – anywhere – else, but he had no luck.

Debbie Li, for all of her talk, could not design a simple electric circuit, so Edwin had to be called upon to do so for her when necessary – with no thanks from her. But as a result of this he began to develop a reputation in the Company as one who could get the job done in communications. As a result, his projects were mentioned twice in the corporate highlights and he received a written commendation from one of his internal customers.

With these developments, Matt Hansen suggested to Edwin that he pursue his professional license. There were a few licensed professionals in the department who would attest to his abilities when he filled out the application.

"Besides," said Matt, "it will take your mind off of your problems for a while."

Edwin thought for a few days and then decided that this would be a good thing. So he started the process. A year later, nothing having improved in the department, he passed the tests and received his license.

And his Performance Reviews were good.

Chapter 71: Four Years

After all of the years of monitoring the case, Louise Tolston was replaced by Owen Kelly, a former journalist. Edwin kept thinking he had been an insurance agent. He criticized Edwin's newsletter writings as being didactic. Edwin thought of challenging Kelly to teach him but never popped the question.

In the meantime, Denny had completed Catholic high school and was ready to go on to college to study Criminal Justice – simply another term for vengeance in Edwin's opinion. Edwin wondered why he chose that subject and, with some tangential thought, chose to go back to church.

Edwin continued to write for the local Society newsletter, believing that practice made perfect. A few months after he started seeing Kelly he received a national award from the Society for one of his essays. Kelly congratulated him mildly.

At work Matt Hansen received a promotion and went on to the vice-president level. He did not bring Edwin with him. So while Denny started college, Edwin was assigned a new manager, Napoli Giovanni, who seemed affable and professional. Their relationship was good, and Edwin received good Performance Reviews.

Three years passed, and Edwin felt stuck in his job. The only way out, he thought, was to get more education, so he chose an accredited MBA correspondence course which Storm Utility approved. He took the tests in the World Trade towers.

Edwin also joined a group at church for those who were single for some reason or another. He hoped to find someone there. He endured the agony expressed by some of those attending and met Gracia Alfano and her son, Walter, who also had been hospitalized with mental illness. He also met Tristan Fasani whose husband had died. She had training as an art therapist and wrote a paper relating to schizophrenia. Both were originally from Italy.

As for Sasha, she and her husband were living in Pennsylvania, and they had another son. They named him Gary. Things were going well for them. They both had jobs and shared a nice home, but nevertheless things had their financial challenges when raising four children.

Edwin was still seeing Doctor Goodman. The doctor shared his obligations with his in-house psychologist, and they alternated the weekly sessions with Edwin.

As good as Edwin's relationship was with Giovanni he decided to switch managers and work again for Joe Nelson, but his co-workers with first-hand experience warned him not to do it. Edwin countered with the remark that he thought he had gotten along well the first time and would make the switch based upon that.

Well, his co-workers were right. There was a growing emphasis on safety in the Company meant for everyone. Nelson contended to his people that it was meant only for those who worked in the field. He went into Edwin's office one day with something to talk about and brought up the subject.

"You will do as I command. Safety is meant only for those in the field. When I tell you to jump, I want you to ask, 'How high?'"

Edwin countered, "If you want a Yes-man, you're going to have to get someone else."

"I will do that."

So Edwin went home with this new burden on his mind.

"If it can be done wrong, we do it here," he whispered to himself.

And at dawn there came a Voice.

"Edwin."

Chapter 72: Whose Voice?

A few days later Edwin called Ruth who was still living with her daughter in Virginia.

"I miss having you nearby. How are you?"

"I'm fine for the most part, but the pain is getting worse."

"Are you working at all?"

"No, the oncologist says I shouldn't, and, besides, I can't concentrate anymore."

Edwin came to the point.

"Ruth, I have a problem."

"What's the problem?"

"I heard a voice."

"What kind of voice?"

"A man's voice. It called my name."

Ruth was silent.

"Were you asleep?"

"Twilight sleep."

Silence.

"Was there something going on outside?"

"This was at dawn. Too early for anything to be going on."

"Well, I don't know what to say. Have you spoken with your doctor?"

"Our session is coming up."

"Speak with him."

Chapter 73: Suggestions for Work

It sounded familiar to Edwin. After Ruth told him to see the doctor he remembered that someone had already told him that would happen. So because he trusted Ruth, he told the doctor. And those stories he was writing for the newsletter, they seemed to have found their way to the TV shows he was watching. But to make sure, he wrote a script and sent it to them. It was rejected, but the communication through the TV continued. He told this also to the doctor. Nothing came of it, and he went back to work on the next day.

Debbie Li was at it again, and Joe Nelson would have no part of it. He sat down and warned her and Edwin that he was going to give both of them written warnings.

"I'm going to lose my job because of this crazy woman!" Edwin fretted anxiously, and he worried about his income.

On another matter, four years had gone by quickly, and Denny graduated from college. His grandparents threw him a backyard party. But Denny was disillusioned by his job prospects. He saw his future in computers, so his grandparents put him through computer school, and he got the job he wanted.

Edwin still heard from Nora, but she was unwilling to meet with him and would not discuss their lives together. She was happy where she was and would not leave.

At work things were changing. The industry was being partially de-regulated, and the Company was looking for ideas to be used in a competitive arena. Edwin was still involved in his MBA program, so he took some time and drew up some suggestions. He submitted them to his boss, Napoli, and let them work their way up. Occasionally he would ask Napoli their status, and they had passed through the hands of Ted Fischer and upward to the VP level.

Then one day a very odd thing happened: Ted Fischer came out of his office. And he swaggered over to Edwin's cubicle to exchange a comment. Then he walked away. Later Edwin overheard that Fischer had won some money from the suggestion contest in the communication field.

Edwin was suspicious. He asked Napoli what had happened to his suggestions, and he was told that they could not be found. So he called Human Resources and told them he would like to see Fischer's entry because he, too, had submitted some ideas, and they were suddenly missing.

"We do not give out that information."

Edwin repeated his story.

"We do not give out that information."

So Edwin called Leon, and Leon gave him the name of an employment attorney who turned out to be too expensive to use his services. And Edwin remembered that he had been told that this would happen.

When he got home, Edwin took a shower, and in his distraction he heard a Voice call his name.

And Joe Nelson wrote a bad Performance Review on Edwin, using it as a weapon. He had said that he would get rid of him.

Chapter 74: Remanded

Edwin, tired of being a second-class citizen in the Court and a *persona non grata* as a whole, sat down and wrote "The Crime Solution" and submitted it to *The Newsletter* where it was published in October of that year. Some other members of the group said secretively that they passed it on to some of their attorney colleagues. At the end of the year, he submitted the article for copyright, and it was granted.

***

Over the wall of the cubicle at work Edwin heard some co-workers talking about the Messiah, and who he might be. They spoke in hushed voices.

"Him!" he heard them say. In a few moments he got up and went to them, but the office was empty. He had waited too long.

That weekend Edwin went to church as he usually did now, and, it being late winter, they sang the Lenten tune "Save Your People." And then when the mass was finished he went home.

At home he stood at the kitchen table and talked to himself, finding humor in every current situation that he faced. Then there was a Voice.

"Only you, Edwin."

To which he chuckled to himself at the absurdity.

In early May he appeared in Court *pro se* as he had been doing. He sat quietly on the seat until his case was called. Owen Kelly was there, and he had brought someone with him.

The judge entered the courtroom, and everyone took his place. They entered their appearances, and the Prosecutor, Patsy Arpin still on the case, made her usual rambling remarks and submitted the report from Doctor Goodman.

The probation officer made his verbal report including the remark that Edwin had sent a letter to the Pope asking to be an advisor. He introduced a movie producer, the man Edwin wondered about, to the Court. Judge Wood's eyes flashed and flamed immediately and refused Kelly to proceed any further. Angrily she cut him off.

It was Edwin's turn now.

The judge asked him directly, "Did you write a letter to the Pope?"

"Yes, Your Honor," he said nervously and added, "My co-workers are saying that I am the Messiah."

Judge Wood almost fell off of her chair.

"That's it! I've heard enough! I'm remanding Mr. Potter immediately to County Psychiatric Hospital for an observation period of thirty days. I expect a report at the end of that time."

And Edwin spent the night in jail on the floor of the crowded cell in his suit while awaiting transportation.

Sixteen years had passed since Edwin was discharged from County Hospital.

Part 6 (of 8)

Second Release from County Psychiatric Hospital

Chapter 75: Nora's Anxiety

Nora let the phone ring until the answering machine picked up, and she left her anguished message.

"Edwin, this is Nora! I haven't heard from you. Are you all right? Please call me!"

She hung up and turned to her mother.

"I don't know where he is. I sent him emails. I left him telephone messages. Where is he? It's not like him. I'll write him a letter. That's the last thing that I can think of."

Chapter 76: Ted Fischer's Interview

Ted Fischer seated himself uncomfortably before the Human Resources representative.

"Tell me, Mr. Fischer, where you got these ideas that you submitted to the suggestion program."

"I came up with them myself," he said haltingly. "Why?'

"Because I received a call from an Edwin Potter in your department who said that he also submitted ideas to the program and wanted to know what happened to them."

"Well, he's nothing but a trouble-maker. Look at his Performance Reviews. And he has a written warning against him."

"We looked at his reviews, and they were very good until the last one that you signed. Can you explain that?"

"I don't have to take this. Mr. Potter is no longer with the Company."

"You're right. He's in a psychiatric hospital! And your performance as department head has been wanting. I want your resignation by the end of the day, and I hope he doesn't sue us."

"What am I going to do without a job?"

"Explain it to your wife and children."

Chapter 77: Back on Admissions

Amid the din that was common on a psychiatric ward the insurance adjuster from Storm Utility finished up his last form and packed things away, assuring Edwin that everything was going to be all right. It was decided that any payments that would be made would begin after the competency hearing in thirty days. It was certain now that Storm Utility knew his psychiatric history and Court involvement. Edwin returned to the TV room and sat on the couch with nothing else to do, also common in psychiatric hospitals.

The weekend arrived, and so did Edwin's parents.

"I brought a book for you to read. We got it from your house. The hospital called us and told us you were here," said Derek. "What happened?"

"I don't know what happened. I thought I was doing well."

"You have to be careful. You can't just go around thinking there is nothing wrong with you. You have an illness. Are you taking any medication?"

"They put me on something when I got here."

"How about before that?"

"The doctors always said there was no indication for it."

"Well, they were wrong."

"All right!" broke in Ellen, "before we get into an argument. Ed, do you know someone by the name of Nora Rodriguez? I have some air mail letters addressed to you from her, and there are several messages from her on your answering machine. Here are the letters."

"Yeah, I've known her for six years."

"It sounds like she is trying to get in touch with you. She doesn't know where you are. I can send emails for you if you write them."

"OK."

"OK, so I'll tell her that you're alive and well but living in the hospital."

"OK."

"Do you have her email address?"

"Yes," he said and gave it to her.

"We also hired a new attorney for you: Michael Fuller," said Derek. "The other guy couldn't keep his billing straight."

"He always made time for me, though."

So that was Sunday. On Monday the psychologist Doctor Steven Becker came to talk with him about the upcoming hearing.

"Mr. Potter, the judge wants an evaluation performed with a report written and submitted to the Court by the end of this month. That's pretty fast, but we are going to have to meet that deadline. I want to begin this Wednesday. Have you seen the psychiatrist?"

"Yes, she put me on medication."

"Was that Doctor Wellington?"

"Yes."

"How are you handling that?"

"I'm drowsy, and I'm constipated."

"I'll talk with her and maybe she can make an adjustment to your medication."

"OK."

"How are your thoughts? Do you still think you're the Messiah?"

"No. People were telling me that I'm the Messiah."

There was a hesitation by the doctor.

"I'll see you on Wednesday."

Doctor Wellington made her rounds the next day and stopped to visit Edwin.

"How long have you been in the hospital?"

"Since last Tuesday."

"I understand that you are having some side effects from the medication. I will reduce the dosage, and I will give you some other medication to help as well. Overall, though, you are responding well to the medication. If you remain stable in a few weeks I will recommend your release to the judge.

That was easy.

And as promised, Doctor Becker came to see Edwin on Wednesday and gave him a brief battery of personality tests.

"I will write my report and make my recommendations. See you in Court!"

Chapter 78: Competency Hearing

Judge Wood entered the courtroom and seated herself at the bench.

"Enter your appearances, please."

"Patsy Arpin, Assistant Prosecutor for the State."

"Owen Kelly, County Probation Department."

"Michael Fuller, counsel for Edwin Potter."

"I have a report from County Psychiatric Hospital submitted and signed by Doctor Lora Wellington. Let's mark this into evidence as C-1," said Judge Wood. "I see some other people in attendance today. Can I ask you to identify yourselves?"

"We're Edwin's parents," said Ellen.

"I see a few other people here as well."

"They have nothing to do with this, Your Honor. Just my husband and me."

"OK... Is there anything that you want to say?"

Ellen spoke up, "This could have been avoided. We could see that there was something wrong, but we didn't know what to do. We were not asked to be a part of this."

There was silence while the judge thought.

"All right then. Prosecutor you may proceed."

"The State calls Doctor Wellington to the stand."

Doctor Wellington took the stand. It seemed to be more of a criminal proceeding than something for someone who had an illness – the crime of mental illness!

The Prosecutor went briefly through the report, pointing out the worst and summing up her remarks with, essentially, an "I told you so." She was followed by Michael Fuller who pointed out only the best.

Judge Wood had a question or two as well.

"Doctor, how often did you see Mr. Potter?"

"I talked with him directly once per week at the weekly team meetings. Additionally, we have trained support staff who live with the patients day and night and enter their observations into the patient's medical chart."

"And what were the observations?"

"Mr. Potter has responded well to his medication therapy and does not show signs of psychosis."

Silence.

"I see in your report, Doctor, that you recommend release at this time. Do you still feel that way?"

"Yes."

"Any other questions?" the judge asked the attorneys.

"No, Your Honor."

"Who is your next witness?"

"There is a report from the hospital psychologist, Doctor Steven Becker."

"Let's mark that as C-2... You may call your witness."

This did not go as well as the inquiry with Doctor Wellington. Doctor Becker covered every detail of Edwin's history and psychosis, each of which could be twisted and turned into symptoms of depravity and symptomatic signs of underlying menacing psychosis. He was on the stand for two hours when the judge halted the proceedings for the day and scheduled them for the morning of the day after next.

It was a long ride back to the hospital for Edwin. In his analysis and experience this was not going well. When he got back to the hospital a cold meal was waiting for him, and the din was in sharp contrast to the silence of the courtroom.

The next morning Doctor Becker dropped by to see how Edwin was handling the situation.

"This is not going well, Doc.'

"I thought it was going very well. Don't worry about all of the details. I've done that for so many times when I appear before the judges here at the hospital. They just want to know the history of the patient."

"This is not going well, Doc. The judge wants to hear a 'warm and fuzzy' evaluation from you."

"What's 'warm and fuzzy?'"

"She wants to hear only good things, otherwise YOU are going to keep me in this hospital for years to come."

"Oh, don't worry about that. Everything is under control. Have a good day!"

And he got up and left.

"WARM AND FUZZY!" Edwin called after him.

The next day everyone resumed their places in the courtroom, and the inquiry continued for the next several hours. Doctor Becker, true to his word, made no changes in his answers. And when it was over, the judge continued Edwin's stay in the hospital for the next year giving him only a move up to a less-restrictive ward but no freedom to move about on his own. She did, however, give his parents the allowance to call the court if they saw anything worrisome.

"I must protect Society!" claimed the judge.

Chapter 79: Frank Kirkland

In the darkness of one hot July summer night, a police car from the department of Health and Human Services drove past the main doors of County Psychiatric Hospital and pulled up to the doors of the Admissions wing. There the two officers got out and helped a man chained and maybe in his fifties get out of the car and into the intake office.

"What's your name?"

"Frank Kirkland."

"Where are you coming from?"

"The jail," said an officer.

"What brings you here?"

"How should I know? Being mentally ill, I guess."

"His mother says he shows signs of breakdown," said the officer.

"We'll make a note. Miss T! Show the officers where to bring him."

"Where is that?"

"Ward eighteen. We can't put him on twelve because one of the patients started a fire, and the place is full of smoke damage."

"OK."

"For safety's sake, we'll assign someone to suicide watch. You can take the first duty until your shift is over."

Miss T led the officers away, and then kept watch until her relief arrived. He looked in on Kirkland for a few hours, and then set himself to snooze for a bit so he could be rested for his day job.

Just as the sun began to rise the man's relief arrived, a woman.

She gasped, "Are you watching him?" and looked in the room with a horrific scream. Her screaming didn't stop. The man tore open the door and untied the lifeless body from the ceiling. Soon others began to arrive to help. Frank Kirkland, though despite all of their efforts to revive him, was dead.

Litigation would ensue for a breach of trust.

Having heard the news about Kirkland and overwhelmed by his own situation, Edwin sat on the edge of his bed, alone in his room while tears streamed down his cheeks as he cried bitterly to himself.

"He was a fucking drug addict! Why does it bother me so much?"

Such a waste of a life.

Chapter 80: Visitations

"Edwin?" cried one of the staff who soon knocked on his door. "Edwin, you have a visit."

It was his parents. It was always good to have a visit even though nothing much happened. This time they brought him a sub sandwich as well as an email from Nora.

"I had to open your mail so that I could take care of things. I hope that you don't mind. A lot of things are happening right now," said Ellen. "Was there an insurance adjuster here?"

"Just before the hearing."

"Well, some good news. They're going to be sending you disability checks. You're also going to have an interview with Social Security so that they can start disability payments as well. Also we asked the attorney to request that your child support obligations be stopped while you are in the hospital. What do you want to do with your house?"

"I-I don't know!" he stammered.

"Well, think about it, but we'll need an answer."

And then there was the small talk. Denny found a job as a computer analyst and liked it very much.

Hope Gavin was still employed by the hospital now as a supervisor and happened to stop by on the ward. She came over to say hello and ask how things were, sorry to see Edwin in the hospital, though. Derek asked if there had been any changes in understanding mental illness and its treatment.

"The last time we were here the blame was put on parental upbringing," said Derek.

"Yeah, yeah! You're right! We alienated a lot of people. That's been changed. There was a doctor who received a prize for his research. He proposed that mental illness is a chemical imbalance, so based upon that the drug companies are doing research and coming up with new drugs. It seems to be working although only a little bit at a time right now. But it's a start."

Then the hour that Derek and Ellen allocated to themselves was up, and they left to see him the next week.

Time passed.

Around Christmas time there was a surprise: Lucinda stopped by with Cheryl, and Edwin gave his daughter a big hug.

"How did you find me?" asked Edwin.

"I stopped receiving checks for child support. So I called the Court and asked them what the story was, and they told me you were here. Cheryl misses you."

With a moment's hesitation to absorb Lucinda's story, Edwin asked Cheryl what was new.

"The Yankees won the World Series!"

"Is that your favorite team?"

She nodded her head.

"Who's your favorite player?"

"Derek Jeter."

Then they talked a little more about sports and his interest in football.

"She started high school back in September," said Lucinda.

"Good for you!" encouraged Edwin. "Any ideas about what you want to do when you graduate. Those four years pass by like greased lightning."

"Either a teacher or a psychologist."

Edwin kept his mouth shut about being a psychologist.

"Are you looking into it at all?"

"I might be a camp counselor next summer."

"Good for you!"

"You can call her on weekends if you'd like," said Lucinda. "Here's her number."

And so the visit went well.

During this season, too, Derek and Ellen pressed Edwin for a decision whether to sell the house.

"Yes. I don't know how long this judge is going to keep me here."

"Do you want us to sell the furniture, too?"

Edwin was close to choking. This was all he had.

"The lawyer says the State is going to take all of the proceeds from the sale to help pay your hospital bill," said Derek.

"What can I do? It's all I have."

"Not much. Can you afford to keep it?"

"Can't you put it in your basement?"

"We don't have room for that!"

"Where am I going to live?"

"You'll have to live in the street, I guess. Then you can walk to the capital and thank our State legislature personally."

Edwin sighed heavily.

"Sell it all."

And in a few months everything he had was gone.

A year passed since the last hearing, and June rolled around again. The judge committed Edwin to another year of hospitalization but with a decrease in restrictions. He was allowed now to go out on escorted walks on the grounds of the hospital which included church on Sunday in the main building.

One day a patient ran away from the group, down the long hill to the train station only to be found by a staff member coming to work who offered him a ride back, which he accepted.

And as it had become her habit, Lucinda brought Cheryl for a visit at this time of year to celebrate Father's Day and Edwin's birthday.

There was a special surprise, too, this June. Denny had married his girlfriend, Stephanie, and they had their first child,

Mabel – Edwin's first grandchild! – in August. Stephanie, though had a daughter, Jennifer, from a previous relationship. Denny eventually adopted her.

   And the seasons changed. Fall came and the trees turned the beautiful colors of autumn, but beauty did not bring happiness to many of the patients. December came with season's greetings, and Lucinda brought Cheryl for her visit with her father. Then there was spring and then summer. Lucinda brought Cheryl for her father's birthday and Father's Day combined. Not much else happened in between, so it was a blessing for Edwin to see his daughter.

Chapter 81: Other Activities

June rolled around, and it was time again to see the judge. Judge Wood allowed Edwin to move to an open ward and have grounds privileges and unescorted walks as well as visits back home with his parents. Denny had married, you remember, and moved out. Otherwise Edwin could not go far. The opportunities were few, but it was better than being cooped up on a locked ward.

And Edwin thought about this slow process. In the 1800s this would have been fine. But this was the twenty-first century, and there was medication now to address the illness.

Although he never thought it would happen, Edwin found there was one therapy that he enjoyed: horticulture. There they grew onions, tomatoes, and cucumbers. In the winter and the spring they made floral arrangements. In the winter they grew poinsettias and sold them to the public. There were regular customers from the outside all year long. Too bad the therapist retired. It brought about the end of the program.

Moving to a different ward also meant having a different doctor, in this case, Doctor Medina. After the Court Order was received in July and Edwin was moved to the new ward, the good doctor stopped in to see him. He explained that he knew Judge Wood, having appeared before her many times, and although Edwin appeared to be well, the judge would not move quickly to set him free. The doctor proposed that he would like Edwin to stay in the hospital for another year "so that he could get to know Edwin."

Edwin's heart dropped. Another year in this vast human wasteland was not what he wanted.

Edwin noticed after a few weeks that he did not see the doctor anywhere. He was told that the doctor went to Italy on sabbatical for at least a year. Would Edwin have to wait for the doctor to return from his trip? In a few weeks he had his answer: another doctor was assigned, Doctor Carmela Abbot. She seemed willing to recommend Edwin's discharge and began to set a plan into motion starting with team meetings and action by the social worker.

The difficulty with discharging Edwin with support services from the State or the federal government was his status with the Court and the circumstances surrounding his case. The social worker was stumped.

So while all of this thinking was going on, the hospital had arranged for a circus to come in July with open invitations to the public as well. Edwin decided to go, and he enjoyed it. It was like a trip back to his childhood when he saw his first circus at the old Madison Square Garden. And a month later in August the hospital held a small carnival. Wow! Who was paying for all of this? But it really elevated the mood of the patients.

In September there was good news. Although Edwin corresponded with his school about being in the hospital and no longer able to attend to his business degree, the school informed him that he had completed enough requirements to receive a certificate which they enclosed. Good news!

Then it was Christmas again, and Lucinda brought Cheryl for a visit.

Shortly after the visit there was another hearing. This time Judge Wood allowed Edwin to be moved to a co-ed cottage on the hospital grounds. These were specially built twenty years ago to help patients adjust to a normal setting.

There were a kitchen, dining room, living room, and four bedrooms with room for eight patients. The biggest argument was what channel should be tuned on the TV.

A nutritionist visited the cottage once per week to instruct the patients on how to feed themselves properly. Some patients had the idea that a good meal was a greasy hamburger with a soda chaser and a bag of chips.

It was here in the cottage that a psychology intern asked Edwin to take another IQ test. Edwin groaned that he had already taken two. She asked him to play along.

"Fine. Are you going to give me the results this time?"

"What? Oh – yes, of course!"

"I like the elephant puzzle. Is that still part of it?"

In a few days before Christmas he took the test, and, true to her word, the intern came back in a week with the results. In some areas he was average, and in some other areas he stood out. But his overall score indicated that he was in the 99.9th percentile, meaning only a small handful of people were smarter than he was.

So Edwin glowed as he had in qualifying to join the Society. All of his life of believing that he was a nebbish, a nothing, was beginning to be wiped out.

Chapter 82: Discharge

In March Edwin's third grandchild – a boy, Bruce – was born. Denny visited Edwin in the cottage along with the family – Sasha and her family as well as Derek and Ellen – and brought him the photo to see and to keep, but to be stored in a safe place at home. He also brought photos of the two girls and introduced his father to his daughter-in-law. Edwin learned only later that she had mental illness in her family.

Doctor Abbot, in another vein, was keeping up her crusade to help Edwin get discharged from the hospital. In her mind it was best to set up all of the follow-up care he would need in order to please the judge. So she assigned the social worker the task of finding a psychiatrist. This was no small task as most doctors did not want to appear in Court.

But the social worker did succeed in finding Doctor Raul Sanchez, and they started sessions in May. The doctor did not take insurance, so Edwin paid the freight. The social worker also arranged for Probation to supervise. The hard part was finding a place to live. No one wanted a patient with a background like Edwin's although other patients not involved with the Court were usually the ones who caused havoc in the community. So his parents were approached, and they agreed to take in Edwin.

And Lucinda and Cheryl came to visit.

In July there was the hearing. Doctor Abbot gave a good report about Edwin and claimed that they had done all they could. At that Judge Wood ordered Edwin's release to his parents with permission to look for a job.

Edwin had spent another three years in County Psychiatric Hospital.

Art work by the author

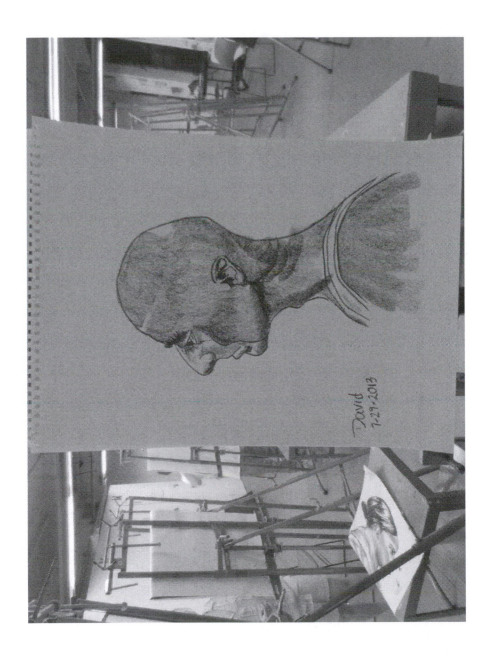

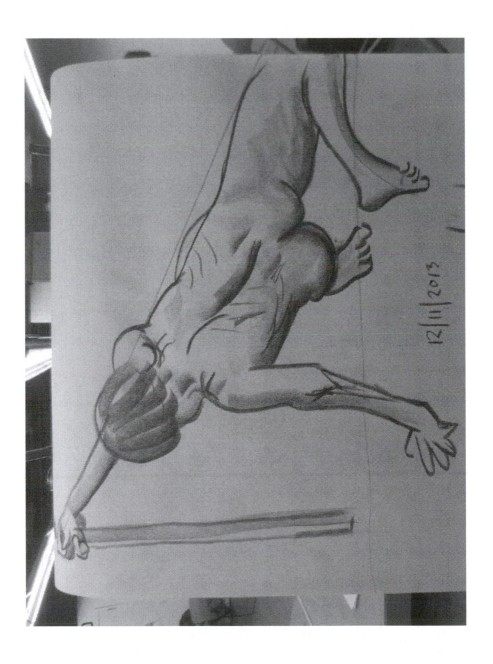

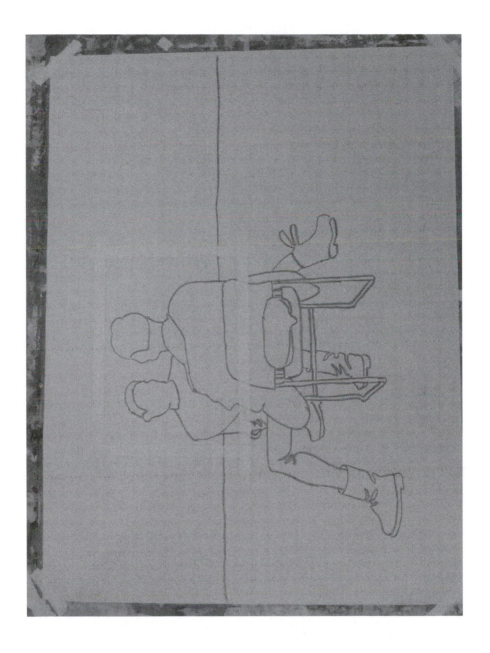

Part 7 (of 8)

The Struggle to Succeed

Chapter 83: Job Search

Now living in his parents' home, Edwin found that being out of the hospital was different this time now that he was forty-nine years old. His children were grown and had no contact with him. There were no love stories he had to tell, either.

His father spoke as they proceeded to their neighbor's garage.

"Proceeds from the sale of your house went toward paying your hospital bills, just like we said. And that's just a part of it. There wasn't enough to pay the entire debt, so they put a lien on your head for tens of thousands of dollars! And the State wouldn't forgive the debt, so they took everything you owned except your IRA which had next to nothing in it to begin with. There's no sense in owning anything. They'll only take it away from you."

There was an angry silence.

"We managed to hold onto your car, though," said Derek as he opened the garage door. "We put it in the neighbor's garage. Her husband died. She doesn't drive, so she had the space... Here are the keys. See if it will start."

Edwin, burdened with the thoughts and memories of trying to make another comeback after getting out of the hospital for the second time, took the keys and unlocked the door of the car. He got in, put the key in the ignition and his foot on the clutch and gave it a shot. The starter cranked slowly, then died altogether. Edwin's heart sank as well. It would be a long road back.

"I'll get you a new battery," said Derek. "Let's go now and get this over with."

They got into Derek's car and drove down the street to the auto shop.

"You're going to need that car," he said. "You're not going to sit around the house and collect welfare. You're going to look for a job."

"Yeah," grumbled Edwin. Of course he was going to look for a job.

They bought the battery, then headed back and installed it. With another turn of the ignition key the car roared into life.

"There you go! That's all it needed! Tomorrow you can buy a newspaper and see what's available. Put the car out on the street."

At that Edwin backed out of the garage and took a ride around the block, parking the car in front of his parents' house when he returned.

The next day his father bought a paper and gave the employment section to Edwin. Nothing there. Nevertheless, Edwin sent out some resumes and interviewed with a few recruiters who had done some good for his family and friends.

After about a month of this Edwin found something about home inspecting and gave them a call.

"In your state it's different. You'll have to call the Committee regarding licensing requirements."

So Edwin did that, and they happened to be under the same Board that gave him his professional license. He asked them to send the information package to him. He found that he could be grandfathered in as he already had his professional license, but he decided to enroll for the training classes anyway. So starting in September and running till June the next year he concentrated on his classes, taking a break only once in a while. He informed Andy Chadwick, his probation officer, as well as his attorney, Mike Fuller, that he was doing this. There was no complaint. He also opened his own business, Overnight Inspections, and applied for the license.

That June Cheryl graduated from high school. It was also a presidential election year, and there came a surprise after Edwin opened his business. The incumbent's campaign called him on the phone and invited him to Washington to be a part of a business committee.

Edwin didn't know what to do. A trip to DC would be great, but he had few resources to make the trip and had no idea how to avoid embarrassing himself in the company of powerful people. He stammered his apologies and left it at that.

A few weeks later they called again. For the same reasons he stammered his apologies. And that was the end of it. He hoped that he would be ready if there should ever be a next time.

And he called Ruth to tell her.

"You give me naches," she said.

Having gotten things in order by now since his release, Edwin tried to renew his visits with Cheryl before she went off to college. Lucinda said no dice. He would have to pay up his child support. He asked his probation officer who told him that was not the way it worked. She would have to hire an attorney and ask the Court to resume the payments, but he could still see the child regardless.

Edwin, still without a job, dropped the subject and began to send monthly cards to both Cheryl and Denny.

In September, Edwin received his inspection license. He told his attorney and his probation officer. Now he could go out and start making customers – or he thought he could. It was at this time, a year after starting pursuit of the license, that both Patsy Arpin and Judge Wood complained to the Committee, telling of Edwin's illness and resulting Court involvement.

"How am I to get an honest job if the judge and prosecutor are preventing me from getting one?" he asked.

The Committee was terrified into action and demanded more information from Edwin. In the meantime, he was not allowed to practice, and he had attorney's fees on top of that now as he had to hire one to address the Committee. Michael Fuller made the recommendation to see Guy Ralphson who had the experience of being on these committees.

So in October Guy responded to the Deputy Attorney General (DAG) and denied that there was any violence that had brought Edwin to the hospital the second time. In January there was a call for an appearance before the Committee. Edwin did well, but no discussion was forthcoming that would allow him to practice. In March of that year he renewed his license though he still had not received word that he could practice.

Chapter 84: Nora's Marriage

The email began:

Edwin, I know that you had asked me many times to meet you, but I never felt that it would be right between us despite my love for you and all that you have done for me. I met a man, Ben, who makes me dream beautiful dreams and my heart sing beautiful songs. He fulfills all of his promises. I am going to marry him, Edwin, but this is not the end for you and me. You are sincere, and you have been patient and kind, qualities that are not easy to find. I will continue to write to you and hope that you will do the same.

Abrazos,
Nora.

Chapter 85: Job Search Problems

"How can I get a job if the Court won't let me take the one that is offered to me? All that I have is that car and whatever I have from disability income. The State took the rest when I sold the house. What am I going to do when the insurance money runs out?"

"Look harder!" shouted Derek.

They were in the living room.

"This is how people end up back in the hospital or prison!"

"Enough! We haven't come to that point yet!"

So Edwin made some half-hearted attempts to find a job but with no success. During the summer he was invited to a barbecue by some people in the Society. He had met them while attending Society executive meetings, and he met someone there – an older gentleman – who told him to get involved with a State program at the Department of Labor (DOL) designed to help people improve their job-searching techniques. The best part was that there was no financial cost. Just give back some time to help out the program. Edwin was slow to respond as he was getting some interviews but no offers. In November – a year since first hearing from the

Committee – he took action on the suggestion and started taking the classes in the DOL offices in the next county.

It was at this time too that Guy had made some progress with the Committee who called for a psychiatric evaluation and report. Edwin agreed to the interview and met the doctor. In December the report was prepared and submitted to the Committee for evaluation.

Meanwhile, Edwin still had obligations to Judge Wood, and he and Mike Fuller met with her in January. His parents were in attendance. Judge Wood made it clear that she wanted to see the Consent Order from the Committee once an agreement had been reached. Patsy Arpin, meanwhile, dragged on about something, and Mike Fuller asked Edwin in a voice just loud enough for the judge to hear, "Do you know what she is talking about?"

"Not a clue."

The judge glowered at them but remained silent.

Otherwise his conditional release from County Hospital was continued.

Also in January, having finished his training at the DOL, he began to teach interviewing techniques and had a lot of fun including his personal experiences in with the course material.

Not all was glad tidings. In April his disability income was cut off because the insurance company felt that he was well enough to get a job by this time. So the pressure increased for Edwin to get some income.

For the next year Edwin continued his responsibilities at the DOL and searched for a job. And in March of that following year he renewed his inspector's license. In May he joined a trade association that would help him – as well as others – to get the continuing education credits that were required.

On another matter in May there was a call for contest entries from one of his favorite national religious magazines, and he thought this might be a good place to expand some of his writing techniques as well. There was a small prize of fifty dollars to be awarded, so he entered the contest.

In July he began his job search training at Business in General (BIG). These few groups that he joined were run by people who were out-of-work or previously-out-of-work or interested in helping their fellow men. Some were there to help one make connections; others were interested in providing some training in the modern-day field of job-searching.

In September there came some exciting news: He received a notification from the magazine that he was one of the winners in their essay contest. Sometimes life was good. Publication would be that October.

It was about this time, though, that he thought to reveal his psychiatric problems to Gracia, Walter, and Trista – people who he had met at church before his second breakdown, if you remember, and was only now beginning to see again. It was a burden to live with the truth of the death of his wife, and as all of them had experience with mental illness maybe they could make it easier for him. So one day he asked them to meet all together, and he told them the story. Gracia, in particular, and Walter never spoke to him again. Trista over the course of some several months made conversations with him but that, too, faded away.

Chapter 86: Found a Job!

In his search for a job Edwin applied all of the techniques that were taught to him and kept those that worked best for him. He sent resumes. He asked for informational interviews. ("Just looking for information!") He made phone calls. He networked. He went to job searching and networking training groups. He spent time on-line filling out application forms. He went to job fairs. Occasionally he got an interview.

There was one memorable job fair held in early December in New York City where he met up with his old employer Storm Utility. Past experience with them made him nervous, but sometimes it is better to let them show their colors than to start a fight. The meeting was simple. He gave them his name, business card, and a resume and the experience he could bring to them as a former employee. In return he received her business card.

"We'll be in touch."

"OK! Looking forward to it!"

One hears those lines at every meeting, but you have to play the game because you never know when it will be the real thing.

They shook hands.

After about a week Edwin, to his surprise, heard from a recruiter who had an interview set up for him at Storm. He went to the interview and did very well. One question, though, stuck with him. The Chief Engineer asked, "Do you need any special accommodations?"

Edwin answered, "No." His guess was that everyone knew who he was, but he decided to keep it professional.

And that was the end of the interview. In the third week of December he had a job offer to start the first Monday of January. He filled out the paperwork to become an employee of the recruiter and a consultant to Storm, told the probation officer and his family that he had a job, stopped teaching at the DOL, and in January started the job.

Chapter 87: Moving on Up

There were some similarities between this job and the one some twenty-nine years earlier when he broke down. His doctor, Raul Sanchez, grimaced when Edwin told him. They were both major corporations. These were both multi-million dollar projects, and in both cases it was his responsibility to bring the job to a successful conclusion (or so he thought in the first case). In this latter case it was his job to make it happen because their previous project engineer had gotten in over his head and, seeing the writing on the wall, left for greener pastures.

No pressure.

But this was now the beginning of the Great Global Recession, and it was difficult for anyone anywhere to get employment. Cheryl was no longer in communication with her father, so Edwin had no idea where she was or what she was doing. There were only a few hints from her brother, but despite that, Edwin was glad to see that they communicated as brother and sister. It was his one goal for them and, apparently, he had succeeded. She had graduated college that May, but he had no idea in what area. Teacher? He thought he had heard. Despite all of this, Edwin could only do his best with what was available to him.

And his efforts to do his best began to pay off. In October the Company announced that through the efforts of its workforce it had won several prestigious industry awards for providing outstanding reliable service to its customers.

So in November he rewarded himself by buying a new car. His previous one had served him well for fifteen years.

Chapter 88: The Death of Ruth Nussbaum

The sea, where all life began but for others brought tragedy and death, rolled up onto the shore of this seaside community only a short distance from where Ruth Nussbaum lived with the family of her daughter and son-in-law. She was house-bound and under constant care, suffering from the effects of her brain tumor.

Today she was sitting up quietly, leaning against a pillow on this dreary day which only made her ache all the more.

"It won't be long," she said to herself. "It won't be long," and lay back in exhaustion from the pain.

Sarah was just returning from the synagogue with her children and husband, Zack, for the observance of Yom Kippur. They entered the house quietly out of respect for Ruth's condition. Sarah looked in on her.

"Mom, how are you feeling?"

"It hurts. I'm sorry, but it hurts."

"We said a prayer for you today."

"Thank you."

"Would you like something to eat?"

Sarah looked on while Ruth lay motionless.

"Mom?"

Chapter 89: Life Goes On

Edwin had sent a Christmas card to Ruth as he always did as he did not hear from her, but her son-in-law called Edwin to tell him the sad news and asked him to send no more cards. Nor flowers. Nor make a donation in her name to a worthwhile charity. That was the extent of the conversation. And Edwin was heartbroken over the loss of a good friend.

Meanwhile most of the year passed and again in October Storm Utility announced that it had again received recognition for its system reliability. Edwin was certain that his project, too, in addition to all of the other work being done in the Company, was responsible for the awards.

Chapter 90: Edwin Allowed to Live Alone

Another hearing took place before Judge Wood. The request put before her was whether she would allow Edwin to live on his own. The probation officer – now Taylor Reinhardt – had no objections to it. Doctor Sanchez wrote a report in support of it. Edwin had lived with his parents for about six years now and felt that he was more than ready to have his own place. And women did not want to bother with a grown man who still lived with his parents. But there was something different at this hearing.

"Patsy Arpin is no longer the Prosecutor," said Mike Fuller. "She was asked to leave. Jay Cole took her place."

The judge entered the courtroom, and the hearing began after the usual formalities.

"Do you know, Prosecutor, whether Mr. Potter's employer knows of his condition and involvement with the Court?"

"Yes, Your Honor. They do."

"But they keep him on anyway?"

"Apparently so, Your Honor."

The judge thought, then changed the subject.

"Mr. Fuller?"

"Your Honor, my client would like to make the request today to move into his own apartment. We have reports from both Probation and the treating psychiatrist that they have no objections."

"I'm concerned about supervision," said the judge, "and I will require that he remains in-county and will continue to report weekly to Probation, the doctor, and to see his parents each week. Who is his employer?"

"There have been no changes there, Your Honor. He is still working as a full-time consultant to Storm Utility."

The judge thought.

"All right. I will grant Mr. Potter's request to find himself a place to live in-county, subject to the approval of his probation officer."

A breath of fresh air.

So at the first opportunity Edwin got in touch with a realtor, and they began apartment hunting. Not a house. Edwin felt that would be too big a burden for him at his age and in his situation. Besides housing prices were sky-high and coming down. He would lose his money.

It was not too long before he found himself a nice place in Parkerton. And he could fit it into his budget although it would require a balancing act. So it was in October that they went back to the judge, and it was granted.

Now he had to buy a houseful of furniture which he did through a local discount store.

The bus as well as the train were within walking distance and cheaper than when he lived with his parents. In short, he made it happen.

And for the third year in a row the Company won the recognition awards.

And in that October, having settled in, Edwin thought about the Voice ten years earlier. Was there a voice? What did it tell him to do? Nothing! "Only you, Edwin." Only you, Edwin – what? Edwin thought and came to the conclusion that regardless he had a story to tell. He would call it In the Matter of Edwin Potter. And he began to organize. He would dedicate it to Ruth.

He began to write.

Chapter 91: The Dating Game

It was a rough world, the dating game. Edwin did not have to say anything about his illness or involvement with the Court to enrage his date. In the few cases where he did, he found that those with mental illness in their families were generally those with the least patience with him. Then there were those memorable comments.

"You belong to the Society? I didn't ask for this! It's over!"

Or…

"I am a genius," she said.

"Oh, did you take the Society test?"

"No."

"Then how do you know?"

"I just assume I am."

Or after a good meal and some conversation (never before the meal):

"I like money. Here is a list of my favorite vacation islands. When will you be taking me there?"

Or from a woman who spent a number of years in D.C. and was now in the Big City to build her fame and fortune by working on engineering projects...

"Engineers this! And engineers that!" And on and on.

Finally, Edwin asked, "So what do you think about me?"

To which there was no reply. She called him the next day, but he ignored her.

But people on dating websites – if you can withstand the vitriol and abuse – are not all bad. Sometimes there is a good one. Helena, for example.

Edwin and Helena had exchanged secure emails for a few weeks, and he thought it was time to invite her to coffee. She agreed, but he would have to pick her up as she had no car. Usually this is an omen of bad tidings, but in this case she was an author from Eastern Europe visiting her daughters here in the U.S. So he overlooked the lack of a car and drove to the rendezvous point as she did not want him to come to the house. Ah! This set up red flags, but he went anyway. He had been through worse.

So as he sat in the car that December he saw 'way off in the distance a small figure trudging toward him through the snow. Soon he decided to call her to verify it was she, and it was. She got in the car. They exchanged some pleasantries, and away they went to the converted rail station that she had suggested.

They had a good time.

Chapter 92: The Committee's Decision

Guy Ralphson had worked hard at negotiating with the Committee. Seven years had passed since the filing of the complaint. During that time Edwin, too, pointed out that the Committee wanted to be able to call the shots in his treatment as well as did the Superior Court.

"Who's primary?" he asked.

So Guy went back to the negotiating table.

After all of this time, however, an agreement was reached and filed that December. Edwin could keep his license, but he would have to put it on inactive status and not do any inspections.

And Judge Wood was apprised.

It was a good thing that he had a job with Storm.

Chapter 93: Job Searching Again

That December Edwin also finished his contract job with Storm Utility. What would happen now? Well, good news for him, his contract was extended, and he was assigned new duties. But he was never comfortable that this would be permanent – and neither were his co-workers. They suggested to him to look for a permanent position somewhere, either within the Company or outside. So he began his search.

In February of the following year he found a promising opportunity as Project Manager for a consulting firm in Kansas City. He was their primary candidate. A twenty-two percent increase in pay with eighty percent of his current living expenses. A recruiter found it for him, but a hearing was required to let him go on the interview out there.

Judge Wood would allow him to go, but Edwin had to reveal his illness and Court involvement before she would do so. So after the hearing Edwin and Taylor Reinhardt as witness found a room with a speakerphone and called the recruiter who had been waiting for Edwin's response to the opportunity.

"This is Kimberly."

"Hi, Kimberly. This is Edwin Potter. I promised that I would get back to you today about the interview in KC. I have good news and bad news. The good news is that I can go to the interview. The bad news is that I have to tell you about a situation that I am involved in.

"I have schizophrenia, and many years ago it resulted in the death of my wife and serious injury to my son. The result is that the Court monitors my case, and the judge has required that I tell this to you. I have my probation officer, Taylor Reinhardt, here to make sure that I did so."

Taylor spoke up to confirm that what Edwin said was true.

"Is your client still interested in bringing me out there?" asked Edwin.

"I'll have to get back to you."

And they hung up, but Edwin had made the effort and did what the Court required.

"I've asked this before of my probation officers: What are you – or the judge – going to do to help me get through this transition?"

"There is only so much that we can do."

"Can any of you put in a good word for me?"

"I'll talk with the judge and let her know that you informed the recruiter."

And he left.

The next day Edwin received a call from Kimberly letting him know that her client was still interested in bringing him out to KC. So Edwin informed Mike Fuller and Taylor. Permission was granted. Trip arrangements were made, and Edwin went to the interview.

In a few days he received word from the recruiter.

"Our client declined to make an offer."

And that was that.

The next month Edwin closed his business checking account for Overnight Inspections.

Also during March Edwin received a call from the president and owner of the recruiting firm asking him what had happened with the Kansas City interview.

"They say you have a tic," she said.

"That's only in the movies."

"Never mind. Do you think this situation will ever happen again?"

"Only the judge knows what the judge is going to do, but I believe she will involve herself every time as she did here."

"Well, then. There is nothing more that we can do together to get you some employment. I'm sorry. Good-bye."

Edwin told Taylor about it at his next report.

"Why did the judge let me go on the interview if she had no intention of ever letting me take the job?"

"You don't know that."

Edwin chuffed in exasperation.

In the meantime, a project came up at Storm Utility having to do with solar flares and the detection of their effects on bulk power transformers.

"You have all been specially chosen to work on this project because of your past performance," said John Timothy, the Project Engineer. "Edwin, you are Lead Engineer.

"The problem is that the flares could cause the unit to overheat and actually cause it to melt – but I doubt that we will let it go that far. So our job is to install a monitoring system on fifteen units to provide information to the control center for their action.

"The caveats include that, one, it must be done by May 31, one-and-a-half years from now, because of our summer hands-off policy, and, two, it will not be extended because the solar cycle will peak at that time, and it will not come around again for another eleven years. So we will have wasted our money if we don't get it done now.

"We have an off-the-shelf vendor item, and we have a sketch of the system. We'll need the numbers from Estimating, but we figure the cost of the project will be about four million dollars. Any questions?"

There were none, so the details were discussed.

Chapter 94: Sunspots and Solar Flares

Six months had passed. Many things had happened on the project at Storm: redesigns at the command of the managers despite Edwin's insistence that there was a standard design from the beginning, arguments both professional and personal. But, most important, time was lost. John Timothy came to him.

"I had to write a Lessons Learned. What's the status of the project?"

"Equipment is ordered. I made a multi-purpose chart to show the current status of what is done and what is not – with dates – and put it on the public domain. We had to ask the vendor to redesign his cabinet. That is about done. I also had to ask Design to go back and redesign the installations because of all of the changes. I need you to speak to the Area Managers about what order you want to do these. Then we can get Design going on that list. At least there is a shot that we can get some of them installed for show. I'll review and sign the drawings along with the supervisors. Don't forget that they just changed their software package so that may slow us down. Their supervisor says he's going to take Indira off of the project and give someone else a chance at it. That means I – me! – I will have to train somebody new and still try to meet the deadlines."

"The VP wants this one. Make it happen."

And he walked away.

Edwin had not been good at handling this type of pressure in the past. Would he be able to handle it this time?

Chapter 95: Helena

Edwin sat in his car at the end of the snow-covered street. At the far end he saw a figure trudging through the snow in his direction. It was Helena.

"I want to tell you something," he said after she got in the car.

"What is it?"

"I have mental illness."

"What kind?"

"Schizophrenia."

"Does that mean you are sad?"

"No. It means that I don't interpret reality correctly."

"Hmm. I know of this."

"Do you still want to be friends?"

"Yes! Yes! Of course!"

"Thank you. To change the subject, I'd like to talk with you a little bit about publishing my book. I know you've had some success in Ukraine."

"I work with an editor. I write, write, write. Then I send it to her for her comments."

"You're self-published, though. You do all of the hard work: write, interviews, TV, radio, publicity."

"Yes."

"I'd like to try the traditional way here in America first: write the story, send it to a publisher, reap the rewards."

"If only it were that easy."

"So I sent the book to a Big Six publisher and a small press."

"And?"

"The big one told me to get an agent. The little one I never heard from – and salvation for criminals are what they say they specialize in."

"Try another."

"As you say!"

Chapter 96: Another Job Opportunity

In August there came a call at home from a different recruiter.

"We have a job opportunity with a utility in Massachusetts. Are you interested?"

"What is it about?"

The recruiter mentioned a project manager position with what turned out to be a fifty percent increase in pay.

"Who would be my employer?"

"We would."

"Any benefits?"

"No."

Edwin thought about that.

"All right. I'm interested, but listen. To save some time, I'm going to have to tell you something."

And he told the recruiter his story.

"Are you still interested?"

"I'll get back to you."

The next day Edwin received a second call. The client was still interested.

"Our client would like to hold a telephone interview either at 9 am or noon. What is good for you?"

The time fell during working hours, but they set it up. He would take the call at his desk. And when it happened, the client made Edwin an offer right over the phone. Edwin said that he would need some time to straighten things out on his end, and the client agreed.

Edwin called his attorney to notify him, and he called Taylor to apprise him of the situation. A hearing would be required on short notice.

Judge Wood granted a hearing graciously, and the usual group appeared.

"I will help you," stated the judge.

After discussion the judge stated that she had no paperwork. So Edwin went home and drew up a letter with all of the details regarding the offer and its confirmation: where he would live and a list of five options showing how he intended to continue his reporting for the Court and submitted it to Taylor and Mike Fuller for a quick return hearing.

It never happened, and as the weeks passed the utility lost interest.

Chapter 97: Invitation

Close to another year had passed –nine years since he was released conditionally from County Hospital. And he sat in the car at the familiar street intersection where he usually picked up Helena. She returned to Eastern Europe every summer to write, and now during the winter she came to visit her family and friends, Edwin among them.

There! He saw a figure again, trudging through the snow in his direction. He so much wished to pick her up at the house.

"Hey, my friend! It's good to see you again," he said as she got into the car.

"And good to see you too! How have you been?"

And they exchanged pleasantries. Edwin came to the point.

"I told you about my problems. We just had a hearing, and, I guess, this is the way it is going to be."

"Well I have something to tell you, too, about us. I love my home country, so I cannot come to live with you here. You can come to live with me at my home! Do you like that?"

"I don't think the judge is ever going to let me do that. She won't even let me move out of the county. Can we still be friends?"

"OK!"
"Then let's go to dinner."

Chapter 98: Meet Angela Bushman

Well, as Edwin did not expect that he could live in Ukraine with Helena, he turned his energies again to the Internet.

"Dear Edwin," began one letter. "My name is Anna. I live in China in a very large city. I love you very much. We must get married right away and have many children."

"Wait a minute," Edwin thought to himself. "What goes on here?"

And as time passed he figured that Anna – if that were her name – was living unwillingly under the Chinese one-family, one-child policy and wanted out to have more than one child. Edwin was not going to go down that road.

There were others who also had some – interesting – stories. One was recently in a body cast and just getting back on her feet. One was suffering from severe depression. One was an Administrative Court judge; that went nowhere. And so on.

One day he received an email (times had changed) from Angela Bushman. She seemed harmless, so he corresponded with her for a few weeks until he felt the moment was right to ask her out for coffee to which she agreed.

And they talked about things: their jobs (she was a nurse case manager), their families (her husband was in a wheelchair since before their marriage and had died several years before, leaving her and their adopted son who was on his own alone), and their situations. She had just gotten her BS in nursing and was thinking about going on to a Master's degree in Gerontology. Angela framed a question.

"The daughter of some friends of mine is getting married in upstate New York in August. She's Jewish. Her mother is also Jewish. Her father is not."

"What about you?" asked Edwin.

"I'm Jewish, too, and I would like you to come with me."

Ho, boy! Edwin had hoped for a little more breathing room before he had to tell her that he was involved with the Court and needed to get the judge's permission.

"That's OK," she said. "It's not a problem. People everywhere have problems, but they have to learn how to handle them."

"Okay, I'll ask."

And Taylor Reinhardt got the OK from the judge. And Edwin and Angela had a wonderful time at the wedding – once it stopped raining. It rained hard for just about the whole trip up and stopped just in time for the ceremony. The bride was beautiful. The groom was handsome. The parents were proud. Who could ask for more?

Angela and Edwin continued their conversation. Edwin told her he was writing a book. She was interested and wanted to know if he knew of anyone who is a writer. He thought of Helena.

"Helena is in her home country writing now. She does this every year and comes back to see her family. For your sake, I think she is losing interest in me."

"Why is that?"

"She wants me to go with her over there to live. Taylor Reinhardt says the judge might give permission with the instruction to never come back if she gives any permission at all. I don't want to do that, so I can't go any farther with her. We keep in touch.

"So, anyway, I'm trying to get my book published. I just sent queries out to two more places: a university press and another Big Six publisher."

"I think you'll do well with them," she said.

"It's not that easy," he replied.

"I think you'll do well. What are you doing for New Years' Eve?"

"It's only August! Geeze!"

"I have a friend who lives in the Baltimore area. Her name is Shifra King. She's a child psychologist. I go down there from time to time."

"I'll have to ask the judge."

"Do you have to do that every time?"

"Yes."

"I will go with you wherever you go."

"For whither thou goest, I will go; and where thou lodgest, I will lodge: thy people shall be my people, and thy God my God:"

Angela finished the quote, "Where thou diest, will I die, and there will I be buried: the Lord do so to me, and more also if aught but death part thee and me... The Book of Ruth."

So Edwin approached Taylor again, and, to Edwin's surprise, Judge Wood said yes.

And they had a wonderful time meeting Shifra and her boyfriend, Mitchell Baylor, who showed them all around the newly gentrified areas of the city.

Chapter 99: Birthday and Art Class

So much time had passed since Edwin's last time in the hospital. Judge Wood had ordered that he see his parents, the psychiatrist, and the Probation Officer on a rotating schedule so that he was seen at least twice per week.

This January it was Ellen Potter's eightieth birthday, and Derek Potter arranged to have it in a local museum.

How everyone had grown! Cheryl was working in a bank with interests in becoming a physical therapist (but Edwin still never saw her). Denny had his own family now with a wife and three children. He worked as a computer analyst for a Big Pharma company. Ian was getting married. Peter was married. Both he and his wife were licensed professionals. Richard, sadly, had called off his marriage. Gary had a degree in theater and was in serious pursuit of an acting career.

Edwin, too, had his own interests. He had signed up for a continuing education class in art in a very good school in New York City. His father asked him what he planned to do with it. If it couldn't bring him money, what good was it? It was just something he wanted to do. This reasoning was new to the both of them.

Chapter 100: Narrative

As time progressed things fell into place. At work Edwin was recognized by his co-workers as a capable Project Engineer. They even got a real alarm with his solar flare project. At first they thought it was an equipment malfunction. At one of the status meetings the Project Manager confessed that he did not know who installed the first system, and everyone laughed because they all knew it had been done under Edwin's efforts.

In the half year or so that Edwin spent with Angela he learned that she had money problems resulting from her husband's death: he had no life insurance. Edwin had married into money problems twice before with the naïve thought that they would work it out together. Nothing of the sort happened, so based upon that he decided to leave her. This did not last long, only a few days. She was tenacious. Still, nevertheless, he promised himself that he was not going to marry her under these circumstances nor was he going to give money to her. Then again she did not leave him despite his schizophrenia or court involvement.

In the meantime, she encouraged him about publishing his book. Still there was no response to any of his queries. Edwin, though, remained confident that he would succeed.

Angela supported him despite whatever difficulties the future held.

"God has heard the cry of the poor. This time He will answer," said Edwin. Angela gave him a grateful hug.

He also sent queries to religious magazines hoping to serialize Part One. Guy Ralphson thought this might be a good idea as Edwin was not getting a response from anywhere else, but this fell through.

A few months later things were beginning to fall apart at work as well. His boss, Jose, (there had been a rotation) took him aside and informed him that his contract was unlikely to be extended. Jose did mention, though, that Edwin had a good knowledge of how the company worked and would help him to find a place.

The annual court hearing was coming up in April. Taylor took it upon himself to read Edwin's book, ignoring Edwin's question, "What do we do with it now?" as there were still no takers. Edwin asked him to "sell" the recidivism study request. Taylor took it to his supervisor who told him to "stay out of it."

Edwin had changed doctors, now seeing a psychiatrist by the name of Tobias Robins. His comment upon reading the book was that he would be the first to hope for Edwin's success, but it was never going to happen. Still he wrote a report to the court favorable to Edwin. Edwin put the book on his bucket list.

Edwin had also gotten a new attorney, Michael Fuller having said that he had done as much as he could. The new attorney was Howard Robertson.

At the hearing the majority of the testimony was that given by Taylor Reinhardt as the doctor and attorney were new to the case. He called Edwin "exceptional." Taylor even went so far as to recommend Edwin's book to Judge Wood for review. He said later to Edwin that this was his first time on the stand in all of his years. He would have preferred to avoid it. The judge's decision was to continue the order.

Ian's wedding was coming up on Memorial Day. Edwin asked Angela to go with him, which she did, and they really enjoyed themselves except that it was still too cold for her. They had to choose between this and seeing Shifra, so Shifra had to wait until the next holiday.

Edwin felt concerned because of the possibility of losing his job. Jose had called him into the office to ask how his job search was progressing. Nevertheless, the Big Bosses at work chose to send him to training. This was a good sign. But the project deadline was coming down to the wire.

And his art class came to an end. By his own say so, the instructor liked Edwin's piece the most.

Chapter 101: How Do You Stir Up Interest?

"I'm not having much luck finding a publisher for this book," said Edwin to Angela. "And I cried today. I don't know if I'm a messenger from God or a man with schizophrenia."

"You're a man with schizophrenia. But as for the book, you'll do well with it. You'll find a publisher."

"You told me that before."

Edwin thought.

"I'm going to change my tactic. What I wrote in the revised article of 'The Crime Solution' – now 'Reducing Recidivism' – I want done as a study, and I need somebody to do it to get some results. Then I'll use that as a springboard to attract a publisher. The reason is that I have no money, and I have no experience at doing such a study. I can run a multi-million dollar project, but I don't have this experience."

"Let a graduate student do it."

"This is an important issue. I don't want somebody lousing it up from inexperience. I just made that same argument about me."

Angela listened.

"Where do I begin? ... I'll send it to Governor Welch."

"Why him?"

"I saw him on the news sitting in a prison with a number of inmates and talking about recidivism."

"What did he say?"

"He's looking for ideas."

"Be careful with that."

"I'm more worried about the judge seeing this as a sign of decompensation."

"Oh – pshwa! You are an American citizen, and you have as much right as anyone else to write to your elected officials."

"Yes. I'll send him a CD with the book on it but print out the recidivism article and see what happens."

"Be careful with that."

So Edwin put his package together and sent it off to Governor Raymond Welch.

Chapter 102: Employment Issues Again

"My second art course starts in a week. This time I'll be doing portraits."

"Have you done any portraits?" asked Angela.

"Some the first time I was in the hospital. They're good, but there is no spontaneity. I hope to develop that this time."

"How about your job? Do you still have one?"

"My boss put in a good word for me in Electrical Engineering, and he stirred up some interest. An interview is scheduled in two weeks for when Peter Morgan gets back from vacation. He likes that I know how the Company works."

"Who is Peter Morgan?'

"He is the Section Manager. He is an engineer like the rest of us."

"What about that solar flare project you were working on?"

"Done! And only two days before the deadline! It works, too. I'm hoping all of this will work to my favor. One issue, though. We won an award for this project – a Team Award – but I did not receive one. People came over to me and said, 'It was your project!' I guess contractors don't get recognition."

"Don't forget my birthday is next month."

So two weeks passed, and Edwin got his interview and received the offer.

"The job is yours if you want it."

To which Edwin said yes and thanked Peter Morgan. He started in one week.

Chapter 103: More Narrative

The day after Edwin received the job offer Shifra came up to the New York City area and picked up Edwin on her way to Angela's. He took the opportunity to let her read the recidivism article.

She said, "I love the concept."

When the three of them got together they discussed what they should do with Edwin's article. Shifra suggested that he send it to The Criminal Justice College to do the study.

Then they all celebrated Angela's birthday. Later, on the real date, Edwin took Angela to a nice restaurant in New York, and they enjoyed themselves.

As for Edwin's drawings, he made copies and gave them to Taylor Reinhardt. Some of them showed real promise. Two were chosen later for display on the school's website. He reminded Taylor that the Court took no action on the recidivism article despite their efforts. What could they do? The supervisor told them no.

As inspiration to Edwin he remembered that Colonel Sanders did not sell his first chicken leg until he was sixty-five years old. Edwin still had a few years left now being fifty-nine.

And Angela came to him one day.

"I heard a man's voice call my name, and there was no one there."

***

The chapter that follows is the recidivism article.

Chapter 104: Article: Reducing Recidivism[1]

I have an idea based upon my experience that may greatly reduce recidivism, and I am asking you to do this study.

Let me first tell you about me. I have mental illness – schizophrenia, paranoid type – and it has brought tragedy into my life and that of my family since 1979. One person died. A child was assaulted but recovered seemingly without problems and lives a normal life. I stood trial in NJ and was found Not Guilty by Reason of Insanity by a jury. I was remanded once to a psychiatric hospital and monitored by the Court ever since 1979, but after the incident I earned a master's degree in electrical engineering and a professional license. I also married again and had a second child. At the time of this writing I am employed as an engineer with a major corporation in New York City. I wrote a book about all of this and more called In the Matter of Edwin Potter (IMOEP) but have not yet found a publisher.

Now let's get right to the point: We need to reduce recidivism, and we need to educate the public that having mental illness is not a crime any more than having heart disease

---

[1] Based upon the article "The Crime Solution" appearing in *Imprint: The Newsletter of Northern New Jersey Mensa*, October 1999. Copyright 2000 David E. Geiger. Used with permission.

or diabetes are crimes. Nor is it something that one can just "snap out of it." Sociologists, for example, would have us believe that mental illness is deviant behavior rather than the chemical imbalance that psychiatrists have found from their research. TV shows and movies commonly portray the mentally ill as murderers and menaces to society. Continuing on that thought, prosecutors in general make the effort to have us believe that the mentally ill are totally inhuman, alien creatures, devoid of any feelings of any kind.

But as for the common criminal -- during the late 1990s when crime rates were falling -- it was said that offenders reacted to disincentives like longer sentences like the rest of society. So what is this about "the criminal mind?"

Deterrents to crime should exist, but as there are well over two million people and counting behind bars in the U.S., where is the deterrent? When crime rates were falling, imprisonment was increasing. If both crime rates and imprisonment were decreasing, then one might be inclined to consider that a deterrent had been found.

From observation I found that a prisoner is generally consumed with the thought that no one gives a hoot about him. In return he does not give a hoot about anyone else. So no one gives a hoot about him. This is the cycle and unless it is broken as it was in the character John Durocher from IMOEP (all names fictitious), crime is going to continue forever.

My opinion is that if we want to prevent crimes then we will have to speak to those who commit them. The idea is that something useful may come of it. Consider the story that came out in 1980, Catch Me If You Can, the story of a check forger by the name of Frank Abagnale, Jr. He was caught eventually but became helpful to the banking industry by pointing out their weaknesses from a forger's point of view. This article that you are reading is an effort to do similarly in the area of violent crime.

Mohandas (Mahatma) Gandhi said, "If a man cannot control himself, then he cannot control his destiny."

But if a lawbreaker should begin to understand this, what is his reward?

"Reward!?" you ask.

Let's start here: When an offender is released from prison, the Court expects – ideally –that he will find himself a good job and live a nice middle class existence. It is not going to happen, and it doesn't happen. We have thousands of years of evidence to support that. He ends up back in prison. This is recidivism.

What is the problem? In my estimation the typical prison inmate does not generally have the skills necessary or hope of ever making it in accepted society. There must be a clear message that there is a place for him if he turns from his life of crime, and we must teach him the skills he needs. What skills? Reading, writing, arithmetic, social skills, speaking English – for a start, and they need someone to trust, a mentor. Most of these guys are going to get out in 3-5 years anyway. Make their time count. Substance abuse is also a problem.

As for the one with mental illness, there can be no real progress until his illness is addressed. In this case there must be money made available for both medication and gene therapy research. Once the illness is under control then other needs can be addressed.

I want to make it clear that these are two different groups with different needs that I am pointing out. It is important, then, to keep prison inmates and psychiatric patients separate because the psychiatric patient is unable to handle himself in most cases.

"Guy Ralphson" is a real attorney who represented Edwin during the proceedings regarding his inspection license, but Guy also works with him on this prison ministry that you are reading here. Guy has the experience of having mental illness in his own family, and he has this to say to say about school shooting tragedies:

I completely agree that the focus should be on identifying and treating mental illness. Until this stigma of the mentally ill as some type of characters in a horror movie rather than genuinely ill people that require our compassion and sympathy is overcome, we'll keep having tragedies like this, gun control or not.

What would make this reduction in recidivism happen? In my estimation there are nine points:

1) reconciliation
2) role models
3) mentors
4) an understanding of opportunity cost
5) education
6) employment
7) substance abuse treatment
8) housing.
9) court-mandated debt

Here is some discussion.

<u>Reconciliation</u>

First and foremost, perpetrator and victim (or his family in the event of a murder) should make an effort to reconcile. The perpetrator must face himself as well as the victim as part of the process.

There was an article by Scott Alessi in the March 2013 issue of <u>U.S. Catholic</u> describing just such an approach through an organization called Bridges to Life. It was founded by John Sage following a 1993 murder of his sister. From the article, a prisoner's words:

Their first priority is getting you to understand what went wrong, where it went wrong, how it affects others, and how it affected you. It just touches a place that other programs in prison, they don't even go there.

Role Models

In the matter of reducing recidivism, we are led to believe there cannot be role models because they would only bring glory to crime. Let me tell you about bringing glory to crime. From my experience the general thinking is that there is no place in our society for those who broke the law. The result is that a life of crime becomes a *de facto* place in society, and crime is, as a result, a foundation of our society upon which multi-billion dollar industries are based. Having no role models leaves it for the drug dealers and gangs to fill the gap for our children.

Additionally, educational psychologists know that people learn by example and imitation. Video games come into question here. This may explain, some say, the fundamental reason for school shootings. Knowing this mechanism, what kind of society should we expect to have when we teach our children that watching violence or playing violent video games is good whereas giving our offenders a good example from among their own and a place in society to imitate it are wrong?

Expectancy theory from organizational behavior helps to provide an understanding about what will motivate a person to do something. The individual needs to see the connection between what he wants and what is required of him to get there. Punishment is a limited, negative motivator.

We can moralize until the cows come home or hard-sell the need for love, peace, and harmony, but these do not address the fundamental issue that if a person does not see something work, he is not going to put any effort into it. As there are no role models for the convict, it is a safe bet that he will believe that, say, education will never do anything for him. His reason is that he never saw it do anything for anyone like him. This lack of a success story creates an aura of hopelessness and leads one to believe that crime and death are the only answers.

Mentors

There is no need to beat this into the ground. Some say that a role model can be a mentor. Yes, but a mentor works one-on-one and can provide the day-to-day relationship and guidance that a role model generally cannot. Maybe a volunteer public with training and experience in inner-city education could be allowed to take part in this. Ruth Nussbaum, a nurse in the book, was an important mentor to Edwin Potter and helped him to believe in himself and to succeed against the odds. Members of youth gangs need mentors and role models and rewards for their efforts to change. Something like Big Brothers and Big Sisters might be the way to go.

Opportunity Cost

Economists should understand this argument. "Opportunity cost" is defined as the next best alternative forgone because once a choice is made from among several competing opportunities, all other opportunities are sacrificed. Here is an example. You have one dollar, and you walk into a candy store to find one candy bar for one dollar and one pack of gum for one dollar. You choose the candy bar, pay your dollar, and your opportunity cost is the pack of gum. You lost your opportunity to buy the gum for which you now have no money.

Now, more to the point, you have a choice to build a new prison or to spend money on programs to help prisoners become contributing members of society. You choose to build the prison, and true to the idea of opportunity cost the programs fall to the wayside. We go through this exercise a few more times choosing prisons over programs, and, boy, those prisons begin to weigh heavily on our pocketbooks. And because crime has not been reduced (the Department of Corrections does nothing more than warehouse the prisoner so the latter will get out in three to five years and commit crimes again), the costs of security systems, prison construction, police departments, annual prison budgets also increase. But it is the choice you made! So our standard of living is lowered.

According to economists we like to spend our money on "our own selfish interest," and this is what makes the economic world go 'round. What would we do with the money if it were no longer being spent on those costs above? We might spend it for medical research (for the mentally ill, say), for scientific research, for environmental rehabilitation, for better housing for the poor, etc., to achieve a higher standard of living.

Education

In today's world of global financial crisis, we are learning that we must educate ourselves out of the hole. According to economists, the poor who live at a subsistence level cannot afford education because it takes money away from the purchase of necessities, so financial assistance must be provided. In the context of prisons trade training is said to be a problem because it is a form of labor market regulation. One suggestion here might be on-line or distance-learning programs for specialized education in addition to general classes for the three Rs and other general training. Whatever works. Start small.

One field of importance is financial literacy. Everybody needs it, but most people coming out of prison do not want to put a whole lot of effort into something that is only otherwise going to get them minimum wage. They would prefer to live on Social Security instead. Teach them how to make their money work for them. Maybe they won't rob banks any more. Or sell drugs. Or pimp women. Or traffic children. And so on. As bad as it sounds, they're only trying to make a living like everybody else. Tell them what an acceptable business is and show them how it is to be run.

Using heroin trade as an example, it is my estimation the problem is not so much the drug users although they rob and beat and steal in order to support their habits. The problem is the middle man. If there were no middle men, there would be fewer drugs available for the users. At the other end of the chain the growers could grow an acceptable cash crop because the middle men would not be threatening the lives of their wives and children if they refuse to grow poppies.

From my experience, education is the only thing that a person can really call his own. No one can take it away.

Court-mandated Debt

There is a report out (2015) called "When All Else Fails, Fining the Family." (Copies available at www.communityalternatives.org) It addresses the matter of Court-mandated fines, fees, surcharges, interest penalties, child support and the like as it pertains to those convicted of a crime. These assessments are placed on them while they are in prison making only pennies per hour for their work. In short, these people are unable to pay the tens of thousands of dollars required of them, and the burden then falls upon their families – who also live in destitution – to help them out because according to the report the inmate is penalized – up to and including re-incarceration – if he does not pay up. A true modern-day debtor's prison. This ruins the lives of everyone involved even so far as to cause him to pursue a life of crime to pay his debts and to support him after release. The result is more prison time and hardship leading to insecure jobs and unstable social relationships.

There are three key findings from the research behind the study. From the report:

1) There has been a surge in criminal justice debt and increasing state punitiveness meted out to those who fail to pay.

2) Families and friends provide important assistance in staunching the debt that relatives or friends face when returning from prison, knowing that such debt can trigger punitive consequences including re-incarceration. This is the main finding.

3) Families and friends should not have to bear the burdens of debt repayment to avoid the re-incarceration of their loved one. Their own situations are generally precarious to begin with.

There are five recommendations to change present policies as well. Briefly:

1) Prevent the accumulation of child support arrears by providing for an automatic administrative suspension of child support obligations for any person who cannot pay. Utilize license forfeiture when there is compelling evidence that accrual of child support is willful failure rather than inability to pay. This is often counter-productive because a person who cannot earn a living wage certainly cannot pay child support arrears.

2) Take steps toward more transparency in criminal justice debt.

3) Jurisdictions should amend all mandatory criminal justice sanctions so that sanctions are imposed on an ability to pay basis.

4) Jurisdictions should adopt a moratorium on the enactment of any additional criminal justice debt until the foregoing recommendations are adopted.

5) Jurisdictions should not adopt new law allowing for additional criminal justice debt without first conducting a "re-entry impact" statement on any proposed law that establishes additional criminal justice debt.

I developed the following outline.

What issues do inmates/Krol[2] patients and mentally ill generally face upon release?

> In common

>> Substance abuse

>> Self-control

>> Debt

>>> *Mentally ill: Lien by the State for years of hospitalization, sometimes decades, leaves the patient in debt for the remainder of his life.*

>>> *Inmates: Court-mandated fines, fees, surcharges, interest penalties, child support, etc. while in prison leaves inmates with tens of thousands of dollars of debt by the time they get out. Families try to help, but they, too, are*

---

[2] A shorthand in NJ for a mentally ill person under the jurisdiction of the Court. Stefan Krol had either blocked or simply never realized that he had killed his wife. After a gradual multi step release, he went to live in New Brunswick and finally linked up with a good therapist. It was only then that he realized that he really did kill his wife and committed suicide immediately thereafter.

impoverished and their resources go only so far.

Poor public image

Reinforced by movies and TV crime shows where the only answer is a violent end.

Relates more to inmates

Can't read, write, do arithmetic, speak English. Lack social skills.

Difficult to gain employment as a result.

No housing (includes Krol)

Must get their own housing without jobs to pay rent

Must depend upon friends or family who may be unwilling or unable.

No social safety net

Nowhere to go in the case of an emergency

Relates more to mentally ill

Need medication

Proper medication may make them feel "cured". Hence they personally decide they don't need the medication and

> *stop taking it. They often break down and return to the hospital.*

Must address illness before any type of release

What are the results of these issues?

Return to former street life, drugs, alcohol, and bad influences

Insecure jobs, unstable social relationships, and financial obligations which – when unfulfilled – trigger a battery of punishments including re-incarceration.

Can't get housing

Ruins their credit

Return to prison / hospital

Give up trying to succeed in society

Public turns against them

What plans/ programs do I have in mind to address these issues/ results?

Reconciliation

Trained volunteer support

Role model

From the prison/ hospital community who is succeeding in accepted society

Mentor

Trained volunteer support

Familiar with inner-city/ prison/ hospital life

Education

Professionals with inner-city training

Programs that lead to GED and beyond

Include nutrition

Employment assistance

Trained volunteer support

Substance abuse treatment programs

Services of physician/ RN and social worker available

Center should also address basic health concerns

Housing

Trained volunteer support

Help from the State to include Krol patients who are excluded from Section 8 housing and residences in the community and must then languish in the hospital.

Relates more to the mentally ill

Medication and gene therapy research

Daily medication

Recommended policy changes regarding debt (see report: Fining the Family)

Prevent the accumulation of child support arrears by providing for an automatic administrative suspension of child support obligations for any person who cannot pay. Utilize license forfeiture when there is compelling evidence that accrual of child support is willful failure rather than inability to pay. This is often counterproductive because a person who cannot earn a living wage certainly cannot pay child support arrears.

Take steps toward more transparency in criminal justice debt.

Jurisdictions should amend all mandatory criminal justice sanctions so that sanctions are imposed on an ability to pay basis.

Jurisdictions should adopt a moratorium on the enactment of any additional criminal justice debt until the foregoing recommendations are adopted.

Jurisdictions should not adopt new law allowing for additional criminal justice debt without first conducting a "re-entry impact" statement on any proposed law that establishes additional criminal justice debt.

* * *

There is a concern about spending money blindly on programs that may not work. There is a mathematical way of minimizing costs and yet getting results that can be trusted. There is a technique called statistical inference, specifically, hypothesis testing. By using a representative sample of a prison population one can achieve a confidence level of, say, 95% in the results of the study. This will remove much of the emotion in assessing the ideas being studied. The use of an independent project manager with experience in this technique is recommended. The study will require educators with inner-city training and experience, mentors who also have experience in dealing with inner-city life, and role models who have tainted backgrounds but are succeeding in accepted society. I am asking you to do this study. A study period of three years is suggested.

Finally, go easy with the religion.

Part 8 (of 8)

A Better World

Chapter 105: The Awakening

Edwin awakened groggily to the gentle rocking of his mattress. Many times more often than not he slept alone, this being no exception. Who could it be?

"Oh, it's you, Lord."

The rocking continued.

"OK! OK! I'm up. I'm up."

And he pulled himself out of the bed.

These things stayed on his mind. After breakfast he thought about other things that had happened in his life, for example, as he rode the bus to work one day in the Big City, the clouds formed a perfect circle. He wondered if he should ask the person next to him if he saw the same thing. He decided not to. What if he were wrong?

Then there was the time when his mother and his aunt were having a conversation in the front of the house. He had been a part of it. His aunt was very excited about something.

"Isn't that fantastic?" asked his aunt. "This is what all of us have been waiting for. And he has a judge in the Superior Court. Her mother is a writer."

"Who is this?" asked Edwin.

"There is a judge in the county whose mother is a famous writer."

"Oh, I know who you're talking about," he said and walked away.

Then there was the time in Glee Club in college where the director was giving their voices a rest. He went through the motion of hitting someone over the head with an iron bar.

"Don't do it!" he cried with a look across the room toward Edwin while he pulled himself back onto his chair. He paused, then said, "And if he doesn't do it, it will be worse... I don't know what to think... Georgie, from page five: Bess, you is my woman..."

And what about his college classmates who sniffed him over, gave him a glance up and down, and then decreed "it" would never happen? What "it?"

Another time he was at a party and listened in to a conversation going on near to him. The speaker, a retired police officer, was talking about someone extraordinary overall but about reducing recidivism at the moment.

"He submits his ideas to a criminal justice college, and they are put into effect in New York, New Jersey, and California – and they work. Holy shit!"

He remembered these and more like yesterday. These things had happened all throughout his life, and he never knew it until now.

Chapter 106: Getting Started

Edwin said to Angela, "I just sent a letter off to the Dean of Research at The Criminal Justice College. Let's see if we hear anything from him."

"OK."

"In the meantime, I have some email correspondence from Guy Ralphson. He is going to take my recidivism principles and apply them to his prison ministry at one of the local county jails. This is how things get started."

"Good."

"I asked him to keep me in the loop and let me know what problems he runs up against. Here is what he wrote.

> Sure thing, Edwin. That I'll do. I've spoken to folks at Prison Fellowship – and the primary problem appears to be the fact that when prisoners are released, there is rarely any follow-up or program in place to keep them on the straight and narrow.

"So I suggested to him that we will need something like Probation School to provide support after they are released. It all takes money, and money is in short supply these days."

"I didn't believe you until I heard on TV some economic experts advocating a new economic system," said Angela.

"Maybe if we have some success with getting these guys educated and on the right track, maybe one of them will come up with an answer."

"Who?"

"The inmates. In the meantime, I'm going to sign up for another art course. This one will be on figure drawing. Here is a work from my last course. Let me show you."

He went into another room and brought back a sketch.

"What do you think?"

"I love it! It's really good. Do you remember Joanne Dempsey? She was the mother of the bride at the wedding we went to when we first met."

"Vaguely."

"She loves your work and wants you to put on a show."

Edwin thought about that.

"As for my book, I sent it to so many places with no luck," he said.

"I have a gut feeling about your book, and they're always right. You'll do all right... If you have some success with your book, I will be there to help you. You can go where you want to go, do what you want to do. But I choose to remain in the background. Whatever happened to that solar flare project you were working on?"

"The team won a Team Award. I got nothing. I'm a contractor, but I put it down on my resume anyway. And that brings up another question: What was the point if both you and I heard the voice of God but nothing else happened?"

After a moment's hesitation Angela spoke, "You were the project lead, weren't you? Maybe something will happen down the road where you'll need those skills, like another job, perhaps..."

"Maybe. I've got to go and see Taylor and keep my appointment."

Chapter 107: What Others Think

"I think your recidivism ideas will work," said Taylor as Edwin sat down at the desk to make his report. "I have a number of years of working in the mental health field before I became a probation officer, and that's what I think."

"Do you think you can find someone to approach the Director of Research at The Criminal Justice College? I have neither money nor reputation."

"Well, I think it will come down to asking the judge to make that request."

"My attorney isn't going to like that. Is there anybody else?"

Taylor thought for a moment.

"Let me see who I can think of. There are studies and there are studies."

"Here, look," said Edwin. "I'm looking for a pilot study, just something that will give us a hint whether this thing will work or not. If it works – good! If not, we haven't lost anything."

"Let me approach the Chief Probation Officer."

Chapter 108: Money Problems

"Angela is for you," said Helena.

"I'm having a hard time with that," responded Edwin.

They were on Skype. Helena was in Ukraine.

"Why?"

"Because she has no money. Worse, she owes money and gets calls in the middle of the night from bill collectors. I went through money problems with my previous two wives. She is a very good woman, but I cannot handle it! I'm seriously thinking of breaking it off."

"She loves you."

"She is going to school for her master's degree and has no idea how she is going to repay the loans. She needs a car. She is renting one now. I am not going to give her the money to buy one because it will only be the beginning of the end. I cannot live with this!"

Chapter 109: Supervisor's Response

"I took your request to the Chief Probation Officer as I promised," said Taylor, "and her response to me was 'don't get involved.'"

"I would just ignore that, but I know better," responded Edwin. "I guess I'll have to find another way."

"Anything else happening?"

"I heard from my daughter! She resents that I have mental illness. This is the problem – one of the problems – that we are addressing in the bigger picture. People need to be educated that this is not a crime – although it will be harder to prove given my present surroundings."

"I'm sorry."

"Helena is in Ukraine. I'm worried about her with the start of warfare in Crimea with the Russians.

"In the meantime I need to look more at The Criminal Justice College web site. I never heard from the Director of Research."

"Good luck with that."

Having finished his report with that, Edwin left the Probation building, walked to his car, and drove home where he turned on his computer. There he sat down in front of it and went to the college web site and began to search. After a while he found something called "research consortium" and decided to take a look. There were a number of institutes for him to look at, so he just went down the list until he found "Prisoner Re-entry." He read it. It sounded just like what he was looking for, and it gave him the contact information of the Director – Celeste Kimball, a woman with a considerable profile of experience. So he wrote a cover letter, made a copy of his book on disc and his recidivism article on paper, and put it all into a large envelope and took it to the post office where he mailed it.

Chapter 110: Emails and Result

It was with much surprise that Edwin found an email response from Celeste Kimball, thanking him for his interest and recommending him to get involved with some local re-entry or mental health councils that address criminal justice involvement. She wrote in part:

> I appreciate your thoughtfulness and broad perspective on the issues confronting people who have been incarcerated. I particularly appreciate your advocacy on the importance of mental illness as a component of the complexity of reentry.
>
> Many of your ideas are components of things that we are working on, and are definitely worthy of study. We are limited in the work that we can do because it all requires that we find special funding... If things are going to change, it is so important that more people be involved in the discussion of criminal justice issues.

"Do you know of such councils?" Edwin asked Doctor Tobias.

The doctor hesitated.

"No, I do not," he replied.

"OK, I'll write to her. By the way, violent crime is down by 4.9% in New Jersey over the past year. As a note, that's when I wrote to Governor Welch with my recidivism article. I'm wondering if there is a connection."

"You what? Listen, I don't want you to write letters to the Governor."

"He is an elected official. He is <u>my</u> elected official. I voted for him – ."

"I don't want to keep you from your rights, but I am afraid that if the judge hears this she will put you back in the hospital. And I am not going to be able to persuade her otherwise... So what else is happening?"

"I broke off with Angela. She and her son have money problems that I can't handle. I think Helena is a better choice, but she is in Ukraine right now dodging bullets. She will be back in the U.S. in March."

"So where do you stand now with Angela?"

"We're back together. Our breakup lasted about a day. I'm not very good at this."

So later, Edwin emailed a note to Guy Ralphson about becoming an expert. Guy's response:

> When you talk about steps to "becoming an expert," I assume you mean paid consultant on matters involving criminal justice? Most experts are specifically educated in their fields (Ph.Ds. in Criminal Justice, for example). I would look at online publications written by experts in recidivism to see what their credentials are. These are the folks you will be competing with.

Also, Edwin found some sources of funding for Celeste's research. One was to approach a state representative who had an interest in the mentally ill. Another was the President of the United States who wanted action taken on criminal justice reform. Howard Robertson, Edwin's attorney, told Edwin to "stay under the radar" and not to write to the President.

Edwin, instead, wrote an email to Celeste.

In Time magazine there is an article about the President who wants to reform the criminal justice system. Maybe you can get some funding there to study the "Reducing Recidivism" ideas.

Celeste's response was:

I want you to know that I am looking for opportunities to conduct more research into re-entry and particularly the mental health aspects of criminal justice. I appreciate your encouragement.

The next time Edwin went to see Doctor Tobias, the doctor was waiting for him.

"I heard from your attorneys. They are concerned that you are having a breakdown."

"Aw, c'mon!"

"No 'aw, c'mon!' This is a serious matter. They say that what you are doing now with all of your letters and emails is the same thing you were doing when you broke down in 2000.

"It's probably Michael Fuller. He's like that. Guy Ralphson is more lenient. He knows mental illness from his own family."

"Let me tell you this: Stop sending copies to your attorneys. Send me the copies. If the judge hears about this she may very well put you back in the hospital, and there will be nothing that I can do about it."

Chapter 111: Pastel Coursework

The pastels art instructor came to Edwin during class and said, "I hope you're not going to stop here with your art development. You have a very good start."

The other students agreed. They said his drawings were bold and exciting.

Edwin thanked all of them, and then told them that he would be having an art show at the school.

Chapter 112: Edwin Loses Job with Storm Utility

Peter Morgan came to Edwin one day at work and told him that his contract would end as of April 17. Edwin's court hearing was two days prior to that, so he told everyone involved with his case.

At the hearing, Judge Wood was very concerned. Edwin assured her that they "had not yet reached the point of desperation." He had money in the bank. He could file for unemployment. And past history indicated that the contract might also be extended at the last minute. Nevertheless, two days later his contract ended, and he began his job search.

The next day after that was Good Friday, and Governor Welch started a program for prisoner substance abuse, saying that the current penal system "has failed." The subject of prisoner re-entry was discussed at town hall meetings.

As for funding for study purposes, Edwin suggested AAAS to Celeste Kimball.

Still in April Edwin brought Angela to meet his sister, Sasha, for dinner, and, with Angela's help, he hung up his art show the following week.

Chapter 113: Pursuing Publication

Still in April, Edwin sent out four more queries to publishers. He also asked Helena if she could write a story that would resolve the conflicts in Ukraine. Although she said she would like to talk with Edwin and Angela, she was waiting for her first grandchild.

Doctor Tobias had his own opinions. He said, "No one wants to see you published more than I do, but I don't believe that will ever happen. I don't want you to get your hopes up."

Celeste gave Edwin some encouragement. Edwin first wrote to her:

> Just keeping in touch. I hope all is well. The book proposal is out in Chicago undergoing peer review by the publisher. No news is good news... Any progress about re-entry on your end?
>
> Have a happy 4th of July holiday. I'll be in Baltimore with some friends.

Then she wrote to him:

Good luck with the book! There is a lot going on in New York. Perhaps you have heard about Mayor Burton Carter's Task Force on Behavioral Health and Criminal Justice. They will be looking specifically at creating better alternatives for people with mental illness who come into contact with the criminal justice system. So cross your fingers that some good stuff emerges!

Have a great holiday weekend. I love Baltimore.

One year after sending his first letter, Edwin followed up with a second letter to Governor Welch. Still no response.

Celeste was chosen by Governor Douglas Ingram for the task force to address criminal justice and mental health issues in New York. Edwin responded:

No, this is the first time that I'm hearing about Burton Carter's task force. I usually listen to the NJ news on PBS. There is an increasing number of stories about successes with the homeless. The mentally ill are sometimes mentioned as well. You know that I submitted some information to Gov. Welch. Maybe someone is taking action on it. You know that Sen. Kyle Brown has an interest in these things.

My hopes are really with the book In the Matter of Edwin Potter. It took me from about April 2011 to September 2012 to write it. (... I believe I started earlier than this. My oldest file was found on a floppy disc (!) and dated August 2010. I moved into my present apartment in October 2010 where I got serious with my writing.) Then I started sending it out to publishers of various sorts which brings us to today. Most of my time now is spent waiting. Let's hope our efforts refashion the way the world handles the homeless and the mentally ill. I believe they will – if we ever get the book published.

On one of my early visits to Baltimore a friend was seeing a community activist who gave us a tour of the gentrified sections of the city. Impressive.

All the best! Hold that tiger!

Assuming this was the result of having previously submitted his recidivism article to Celeste, Edwin thought it might be good to try to send it to a few elected officials. He had already sent it to Governor Welch. So he thought to send it to Governor Ingram which he did. And in a few days he had a response from the Governor. Probably boilerplate, but it was more than he had received from Governor Welch.

In the meantime, Edwin's job search was bearing no fruit.

Angela told Edwin it was hard to get to know him. Edwin replied that it was hard for him to trust people.

Helena was going back to Ukraine for a month come October.

Then there was something interesting on the local TV news.

Chapter 114: Politics

On the local news there was the announcement of the opening of Martin's Place, a transitional setting for those getting out of prison. Governor Welch, the city mayor, a former governor as well as some members of Congress were opening the place with great fanfare, saying this was unique and the only such place in the country.

Edwin wrote another letter to Governor Welch reminding him of the ideas he had presented to the Governor, but there was never a response.

Celeste wrote to him, "We are not surprised, are we?"

"No, I guess not," responded Edwin. Then he wrote, "How are things going with that task force project in The Big City? Any movement?"

Celeste wrote:

Yes, there has been a lot of movement. They are retraining police and send them out in teams with mental health workers, they have an RFP out now to integrate mental health services into other agencies, and a number of other things. You should be pleased.

Edwin also wrote to his Senator and state representative, but there were no responses there, either. But the news was full of stories about crime going down and working with those released from prison as successful efforts.

Chapter 115: Realization

Edwin and Angela were on the couch in his apartment. He was out of sorts. He was getting nowhere with his job search. (He was too old, and, besides, Time magazine had reported that there were jobs for burger flippers and Ph.Ds but nothing in between.) His book was unpublished. And there was one other thing.

"What ever happened to Officer Castellano?" he asked, and tears trickled down his face.

"I don't know who he is," said Angela.

"He appeared on my behalf during the trial proceedings and was shot to death soon after I was acquitted. The papers said it was a gun-cleaning accident."

"Maybe it was."

"So many people died in this case. I think the lesson I learned is that I am not a pawn. It is my life to do as I choose, and, now that I know that, I can do a pretty good job of it.

"Edwin, you planted the seed," Angela said softly.

"Nobody knows."

"God saw it and will remember you."

"No rushing wind? No raging thunderstorms? No pillars of fire?"

"Sometimes he just uses good people. There are programs for prison inmates now where there were none before. And they are working. You told me yesterday that Governor Welch closed one of the State prisons and re-purposed it to a substance abuse treatment center for incarcerated inmates."

Edwin took a deep breath.

"Yes, and he is expanding the program. Very few of the formerly incarcerated go back to prison after enrolling in a prisoner re-entry program."

"They are all big issues. There are over two and a half million people in prison, but your ideas are working."

"Say it again?"

"They're working."

Recommended Reading

Alessi, Scott; Article "Truth and Consequences"; U.S. Catholic; March 2013; pg. 12

Arterburn, Stephen and Jack Felton; Toxic Faith: Understanding and Overcoming Religious Addiction; Oliver Nelson, 1991

Califano, Joseph A. Jr.; High Society: How Substance Abuse Ravages America and What to Do About It; PublicAffairs, 2007

Coleman, Lee, M.D.; The Reign of Error: Psychiatry, Authority, and Law; Beacon Press, 1984

Earley, Pete; Crazy: A Father's Search Through America's Mental Health Madness; G.P. Putnam's Sons, 2006

Fraga, Brian; Article: "Crime Fighter"; U.S. Catholic; June 2012; pg. 47

Hofstadter, Richard; Anti-Intellectualism in American Life; Vintage Books, 1963 (Pulitzer Prize winner)

Klein, Joe; Article: "Learning that Works"; <u>Time</u>; May 14, 2012; pg. 34

McCuen, Gary E.; <u>Treating the Mentally Disabled</u>; Gary E. McCuen Publishing, Inc., 1988

Nagrecha, Mitali et al; report "When All Else Fails, Fining the Family"; Center for Community Alternatives; copies available at www.communityalternatives.org

Nasar, Sylvia; <u>A Beautiful Mind</u>; Simon & Schuster, 1998 (National Book Critics Circle Award – 1998, Pulitzer Prize nominee)

Schwartz, Emma; Article: "A Court of Compassion"; <u>US News & World Report</u>; Feb. 18, 2008

Sheehan, Susan; <u>Is There No Place on Earth for Me?</u>; Vintage Books, 1982 (Pulitzer Prize winner)

List of Names Used in Book

	Book last	Book first	Comments
1	Aaron	Daniel	EP Trial attorney
2	Abbot	Carmela	psychiatrist at County
3	Agnello	Myra	EP first girlfriend
4	Agnello	Joseph	Myra husband
5	Agnello	Gloria	Myra younger daughter
6	Agnello	Randi	Myra older daughter
7	Alfano	Gracia	EP girlfriend
8	Alfano	Walter	Gracia son
9	Allen	Gene	State/ County patient
10	Anderson	Billy	State HST
11	Arpin	Patsy	later County Prosecutor
12	Bailey	Georgia	first County Prosecutor
13	Baker	Michelle	State psychology intern
14	Baylor	Mitchell	Shifra King's boyfriend
15	Becker	Steven	County psychologist
16	BIG (Business in General)		networking group
17	Black	Jimmy	State patient let out the door
18	Bloom		town
19	Breakstone	Roger	State patient
20	Brinkerhoff	Rolf	State psychiatrist
21	Brown	Kyle	State Assemblyman
22	Bushman	Angela	EP girlfriend
23	Carter	Burton	NYC mayor
24	Castellano	Francis	EP arresting officer
25	Chadwick	Andy	Probation Officer
26	Cisco	Larry	Sasha Potter husband
27	Cisco	Richard	Sasha Potter son
28	Cisco	Peter	Sasha Potter son
29	Cisco	Ian	Sasha Potter son
30	Cisco	Gary	Sasha Potter son
31	Clare	Jack	EP school playmate

32	Clare	Sandy	Mother of Jack. Works in jail
33	Coast Radio		EP telecom employer
34	Cohen	Trishara	Ruth niece. Court Recorder
35	Cole	Jay	County Prosecutor
36	County Psychiatric Hospital		
37	Crystal Radio Inc.		EP small business employer
38	Cuccinelli	Olivia	Pastor daughter
39	Cuccinelli	Deangelo	Olivia husband
40	Daley	Shawn	Catholic priest
41	Dee	Barbara	Social worker -adoption case
42	Dempsey	Joanne	Angela Bushman friend
43	Dempsey	Drew	Husband of Joanne
44	Durocher	John	State patient. Threatens EP, then applauds Sunny tune.
45	Edmonds	Desmond	Psychiatrist. Works @ Addison Memorial. Gun issue
46	English	Jerry	"Frankenstein" Escapes
47	Fasani	Trista	Gracia Alfano friend
48	Fischer	Ted	EP Storm Utility manager
49	Fitzgerald	Linda	Adoption atty for Amy Potter mother
50	Francesco	Alex	Potter family attorney
51	Fuller	Michael	EP attorney
52	Gavin	Hope	County Hospital supervisor
53	Giovanni	Napoli	EP Storm Utility manager
54	Goodman	Arthur	EP psychiatrist
55	Green	Willie	State HST. Trombone player
56	Gregory	Paul	State Hospital patient
57	Griffin		Denny adoption judge
58	Hansen	Matthew	EP Storm Utility manager
59	Ingram	Douglas	NYS Governor
60	Jose		EP Storm Utility manager
61	Kasper	Dwight	Prosecution trial psychiatrist
62	Keenan	Glenn	State Assemblyman
63	Kelly	Owen	Probation Officer

64	Kenwood	Ronnie	County social worker
65	Kimball	Celeste	Director at The Criminal Justice College
66	King	Shifra	Angela Bushman friend
67	Kirchganger	Luella	EP girlfriend. Researcher
68	Kirkland	Frank	State Hospital patient
69	Li	Debbie	EP coworker at Storm Utility
70	Luciano	Julius	County psychiatrist
71	Mann	Theresa	Amy mother
72	Medina		County psychiatrist. Sabbatical
73	Martin's Place		inmate transitional services
74	Midland County		EP's home
75	Midland County CMH		County Mental Health Center
76	Morgan	Peter	EP Storm Utility manager
77	Nelson	Joseph	EP Storm Utility manager
78	NLO		EP small business employer
79	Nussbaum	Ruth	RN at County Hospital
80	Nussbaum	Sarah	daughter of Ruth
81	Nussbaum	Manuel	Ruth husband
82	O'Connor	Sherry	County LPN. Friend of Ruth
83	O'Keefe	Ken	EP landlord
84	One Hour of Your Time		TV news program
85	Overnight Home Inspections		EP inspection business
86	Pachaw State Hospital		Jerry English escapes from here
87	Parkerton		town
88	Potter	Edwin	main character - EP
89	Potter	Derek	EP father
90	Potter	Ellen	EP mother
91	Potter	Sasha	EP sister
92	Potter	Amy	EP first wife
93	Potter	Cheryl	EP daughter w/Lucinda
94	Potter	Stephanie	EP daughter-in-law
95	Potter	Mabel	EP granddaughter

96	Potter	Jennifer	EP granddaughter
97	Potter	Bruce	EP grandson
98	Potter	Denny	EP son w/ Amy
99	Ralphson	Guy	EP attorney
100	Reinhardt	Taylor	Probation officer
101	River Road		Street where EP lived
102	Robertson	Howard	EP attorney
103	Robins	Tobias	EP psychiatrist
104	Rodriguez	Nora	EP girlfriend
105	Rosenberg	Leon	EP attorney
106	Sanchez	Raul	EP psychiatrist
107	Sanchez	Dom	State patient.
108	Sanders	Bart	Public Defender
109	Schmidt	Jacob	Director of State max. security Unit
110	Simon	Howard	CMH psychologist
111	Southland		town
112	St. Mark's Hospital		Amy & Denny taken here
113	State Psych. Hospital		
114	State University		engineering school
115	Stein	Adam	State patient
116	Storm Utility		utility provider
117	Tanzer	Lucinda	EP second wife
118	Taylor	Ginny	County psychologist
119	The Criminal Justice College		Criminal Justice
120	The High-IQ Society		a high IQ society
121	Timothy	John	Storm Utility Proj Engr
122	Tolston	Louise	Probation Officer
123	Vogel	Barbra	CMH social worker
124	Walker	Rex	State Hosp. HST
125	Washington	Samuel	Trial judge.
126	Welch	Raymond	Governor of NJ
127	Wellingtom	Lora	County psychiatrist-Admissions
128	Wilson	Max	fellow alumnus of EP
129	Wood	Reanna	IMOEP case judge
130	ZipComm		Telecom company

131	Zucker	Wyatt	later husband of Lucinda Tanzer
132		Zack	Sarah Nussbaum's husband
133		Helena	writer. Friend of EP
134		Ben	husband of Nora Rodriguez
135		Rose	Aaron's secretary
136		Slick	State patient talks gibberish
137		Stan	State patient - artistic
138		Susan	State art therapist
139		Jamal	State patient
140		Sandra	State art therapist intern
141		Scotty	County. Pinky problem
142		Zoe	County patient
143		Ronald	County patient
144		Mandy	County. Friend of Tom.
145		Tom	County. Friend of Mandy.
146		Celeste	Assembler at Crystal Radio
147		Golda	Storm Utility secretary
148		Kimberly	Recruiter--KC job

Q&A with the Author

What is mental illness? Schizophrenia?

Schizophrenia is a mental disorder (also known as a mental illness) as much as depression, bipolar disorder, and autism are mental disorders. Mental disorders include a wide range of conditions affecting mood, thinking, and behavior. Schizophrenia is also included as a brain disorder in which people interpret reality abnormally. These disorders are usually treated with medication. Contrary to popular belief, schizophrenia is not split personality or multiple personality. http://www.mayoclinic.org/diseases-conditions/schizophrenia/basics/definition/con-20021077

From the DSM5 (Diagnostic and Statistical Manual of Mental Disorders) we learn that "schizophrenia is characterized by delusions, hallucinations, disorganized speech and behavior, and other symptoms that cause social or occupational dysfunction. For a diagnosis, symptoms must have been present for six months and include at least one month of active symptoms." http://www.dsm5.org/Documents/Schizophrenia%20fact%20Sheet.pdf

Facts and Information about People with Schizophrenia

From Surviving Schizophrenia: A Manual for Families, Patients, and Providers, 5th ed. (E. Fuller Torrey; Quill) we learn:

- There are over 2.2 million people with schizophrenia in the United States as of 2006, of which approximately:
  - 6% are homeless or live in shelters
  - 6% live in jails or prisons

- o   10% live in nursing homes
- o   20% live in supervised housing (group homes, etc.)
- o   25% live with a family member
- o   28% live independently

What is Life Like with Schizophrenia?

- The average age for onset is 18 years in men and 25 years in women. (Acta Pschy8atri. Scand. 89 135-141; 1991) The earlier schizophrenia is diagnosed and treated, the better the outcome of the person and the better the recovery. (Yale University Medical School)
- At any given time, there are more people with untreated severe psychiatric illnesses living on America's streets than are receiving care in hospitals. (Treatment Advocacy Center)
- People with schizophrenia have a 50 times higher risk of attempting suicide than the general population. Suicide is the number one cause of premature death among people with schizophrenia. (Treatment Advocacy Center)
- People with schizophrenia are far more likely to harm themselves than to be violent toward the public. Violence is not a symptom of schizophrenia. News and entertainment media tend to link mental illnesses including schizophrenia to criminal violence. (For more information check Schizophrenia.com, Facts and Statistics)
- Even when people with mental disorders are recognized as having a medical condition, the treatment they receive is often less than humane. (WHO) http://www.who.int/features/2005/mental_health/en/

What books and articles often miss when discussing the mentally ill is how the latter are often a forgotten people. From WHO (World Health Organization), "people with mental disorders are some of the most neglected people in the world. In many communities, mental illness is not considered a real medical condition, but viewed as a weakness of character or as a punishment for immoral behaviour." (http://www.who.int/features/2005/mental_health/en/) also http://www.inquiriesjournal.com/articles/1428/the-forgotten-illnesses-the-mental-health-movements-in-modern-america

While I was in Trenton Psychiatric Hospital Vroom Building – a maximum-security psychiatric facility – it was rare to see an individual who was lucky enough to have a visit from a family member or a friend. Patients do not have a designated place in society outside of the institutions they live in whether it is a private hospital or state hospital where they are placed by the court for breaking the law. I consider myself fortunate that my family – even my ex-wife – took the time to visit with me.

What is criminal justice?

From The National Center for Victims of Crime, "The criminal justice system is the set of agencies and processes established by governments to control crime and impose penalties on those who violate laws. There is no single criminal justice system in the United States but rather many similar, individual systems. How the criminal justice system works in each area depends on the jurisdiction that is in charge: city, county, state, federal or tribal government or military installation. Different jurisdictions have different laws, agencies, and ways of managing criminal justice processes"
https://victimsofcrime.org/help-for-crime-victims/get-help-bulletins-for-crime-victims/the-criminal-justice-system

The Urban Institute put out a research report dealing with "The Processing and Treatment of Mentally Ill Persons in the Criminal Justice System." It says "severe mental illness afflicts nearly one-quarter of the US correctional population, including individuals in prisons, in jails, and on probation" yet they cycle through the system without appropriate medical care. Our current knowledge on identifying cost-effective programs and policies is very limited with extremely rare, rigorous evaluations of programs and policies directed toward the mentally ill. But the report does present a few interventions and policies for mentally ill offenders:

1) Diversionary mechanisms that route the mentally ill to treatment programs rather to prison or jail.
2) Community-based reentry programs
3) Policies that provide mentally ill offenders with more access to medical care.

http://www.urban.org/sites/default/files/alfresco/publication-pdfs/2000173-The-Processing-and-Treatment-of-Mentally-Ill-Persons-in-the-Criminal-Justice-System.pdf

When I was in Trenton there were reports in the news about "former mental patients" terrorizing the community. These were few, but they were the only ones being reported. This frightened the community and thereby frightened the judges who became loath to give freedoms to more trustworthy patients. And these considerations last throughout the life of the case.

What is recidivism?

"Recidivism is one of the most fundamental concepts in criminal justice. It refers to a person's relapse into criminal behavior, often after the person receives sanctions or undergoes intervention for a previous crime. Recidivism is measured by criminal acts that resulted in rearrests, reconviction or return to prison with or without a new sentence during a three-year period following the prisoner's release." (National Institute of Justice; http://www.nij.gov/topics/corrections/recidivism/pages/welcome.aspx) In other words, a person commits a crime, is tried, then goes to jail. He gets out, commits a crime, is tried, then goes to jail. He gets out and so on ad nauseam.

One example of the issues being considered is "ban the box." (https://www.whitehouse.gov/sites/default/files/page/files/20160423_cea_incarceration_criminal_justice.pdf) You may have seen the box on employment or college applications. Most of us can ignore it and so pay no attention to it, but it is a monumental obstacle to those who have been in prison and want to change their ways. The box asks something like "Have you ever been arrested or convicted of a felony or any other way involved with the law?" This is to screen out those with criminal backgrounds so the business does not have to assume the risk associated with him. Well, let's look at this. If this guy does not get a job he may very well return to crime as a means to support himself. Someone has to take on the risk, and it is not right that the justice system just dumps these guys out onto the street as I saw at Trenton nor is it right for education to be denied to him. He needs the skills to get a job just like everyone else. There is further discussion and efforts about this and more at John Jay College. http://johnjaypri.org/

"National Statistics on Recidivism

Bureau of Justice Statistics studies have found high rates of recidivism among released prisoners. One study tracked 404,638 prisoners in 30 states after their release from prison in 2005. The researchers found that:

- Within three years of release, about two-thirds (67.8 percent) of released prisoners were rearrested.
- Within five years of release, about three-quarters (76.6 percent) of released prisoners were rearrested.
- Of those prisoners who were rearrested, more than half (56.7 percent) were arrested by the end of the first year.
- Property offenders were the most likely to be rearrested, with 82.1 percent of released property offenders arrested for a new crime compared with 76.9 percent of drug offenders, 73.6 percent of public order offenders and 71.3 percent of violent offenders."

http://www.nij.gov/topics/corrections/recidivism/pages/welcome.aspx

One of the reasons why I live where I do is that the judge who oversees my case cannot with 100% certainty ever know if things will happen again. As long as the case is not dismissed the Court still has the power to pull me off of the street if it should see something developing. This is an action of the criminal justice system in practice.

What is opportunity cost, and how does it fit into the story?

According to economists, "opportunity cost" is defined as the next best alternative forgone because once a choice is made from among several competing opportunities, all other opportunities are sacrificed. (Keith Lumsden, Economics, Pitman Publishing, 1991, pg. 1/8) As an example, you have a choice to build a new prison or to spend money on programs to help prisoners become contributing members of society. You choose to build the prison, and true to the idea of opportunity cost the programs fall to the wayside. We go through this exercise a few more times choosing prisons over programs, and, boy, those prisons begin to weigh heavily on our pocketbooks.

I spent a few nights in jail as a result of my illness. I was also an observer at Northern State Prison in Newark, New Jersey as part of a training program given by the Paterson Chamber of Commerce in 1997. In neither case at that time did I find that any of the inmates were receiving training that would help them to decrease their recidivism.

What we have to remember is that if we choose one option, the other issues must still be addressed, i.e., criminal behavior must be mitigated before release from prison.

What is the book about?

This story involves a man suffering from schizophrenia who kills his wife while in a delusion and goes on trial for his life. It is the story of his struggle to regain his place in society and, as a result, lays the groundwork for workable criminal justice reform.

We're talking about the value of a person. Today we see him as a criminal, but what about tomorrow if he gets the proper help and support?

Why did you write this book?

Originally it was a catharsis, and I wrote only the first ten chapters. After I finished, I said "There is more to this story." I did this several times as I wrote until I got to where we are today. If you click on the link to John Jay College of Criminal Justice Prisoner Re-entry Institute, I would say, "This is what my aim is, what my issues are." http://johnjaypri.org/ . There is a newsletter available on the web site under ABOUT. You can also join their mailing list under ABOUT/CONTACT US.

What makes you qualified to tell this story?

I am qualified because this is my story; it happened to me.

Were you ever convicted of a crime?

No.

Is it illegal for you to write such a story?

I checked with my attorney on this. It is illegal for one convicted of a crime to profit from such a book, but I have not been convicted of a crime. There is good that comes from this book.

Why do you include drawings?

Edwin has an interest in art. It is therapeutic, and he finds he has a talent for it. The object is to share them with my readers and maybe develop my skills to a professional level.

Where did you get the idea for this book?

I had a tragic breakdown in 1979 where one person died and another was seriously injured. I developed a friendship with one of the head nurses at the hospital – Herma Darrow. She encouraged me to write the book though I had no skills or experience at the time. She believed in me and changed my life. Sadly, she never lived to see the book come to fruition. She died of a brain tumor from smoking.

Topics for Discussion

1) True story - Edwin Potter has a mental illness and as a result killed someone. He is on trial and facing execution. If you were a member of the jury, how would you vote?

2) What value do we place on a life before we know what will come of it? What if Edwin has the key to bring an end to crime? Would your vote still be the same?

3) Mental health diagnoses are often complex and prone to subjective opinion. How can we use them to help both the individual in question and the society we live in?

4) How important are substance abuse treatment and follow-up care for the mentally ill? Would this also apply to prison inmates?

5) Read the book. Are your answers still the same?

Edwin Potter is an educated, professional, middle-class man with a family and a mortgage – typical of society. But he has schizophrenia, and it ruined his life as well as the lives of those around him. He killed his wife and stood trial for her murder. But the jury decided that he suffered from mental illness and acquitted him. He was released to the community with court supervision after years of hospitalization.

Based upon a true story (an autobiography with all of the names changed), IMOEP is the story of a man with schizophrenia – Edwin Potter – who kills his wife and stands trial for his life. Found Not Guilty by Reason of Insanity by a jury, he spends the rest of his life recovering from his illness and trying strongly to regain his place in society as a professional and as a contributing member of society.

Mr. Geiger, as Edwin Potter, takes up writing to express himself and, with time, writes the article "Reducing Recidivism" (chapter 104 in IMOEP) that addresses the roots of crime and – successfully – how to reduce it. Although Mr. Geiger was initially afraid of publishing his thoughts on this issue, movies and TV crime shows continually portrayed the only solution as a violent end, and he felt something had to be said.

It was during this time – that is, the 1980s and 1990s – that the justice system was building prisons. This was their answer to crime. As we know now, it did not work. We now have over 2.1 million inmates in prison, by far the most in the world, but crime has not gone down. Mr. Geiger, angered by this and being on the receiving end of public criticism, wrote an article - based upon his experience - now called "Reducing Recidivism" which he published in a Mensa newsletter in 1999. There he states specifically why prison inmates recidivate and what has to be done to fix it. In 2010 he dusted it off and revised it into a book which is brought to your attention today: In the Matter of Edwin Potter: Mental Illness and Criminal Justice Reform. In 2013 he sent the recidivism article to his state Governor. (It is available for download on the website www.davidegeiger.com .) In 2016 he published the book and sent a copy to the Governor. Crime is down, and the Governor is expanding the program. This is the story of how it all happened and so much more.

Would this be of interest to the people in your field? How could we make this discussion more relevant? I would like to see this book placed on your reading list. Who can I connect with at your location to discuss this more?

More praise for <u>In the Matter of Edwin Potter</u>

"This along with other issues you cite explains why recidivism is almost inevitable – the lack of education, financial opportunities, social support, and the general climate of prisoners – which leads us to release prisoners with virtually no chance to go in a different direction."

--(Rev.) Frank DeSiano, CSP, President, Paulist Prison Ministries, Washington, DC

Made in the USA
Columbia, SC
26 June 2017